# MASTERING THE MONEY MAZE
## *10 Secrets to Winning Business Financing*

## Diane Weklar

**STARGAZER**
Publishing Company
PO Box 77002
Corona, CA 92877-0100

"Educate, Enlighten, Entertain"

Published by Stargazer Publishing Company
PO Box 77002
Corona, CA 92877-0001
(800) 606-7895
(951) 898-4619
FAX (951) 898-4633
e-mail: stargazer@stargazerpub.com
website: http://www.stargazerpub.com

Cover Design: www.calypsoconcepts.com

**Disclaimer**

Library of Congress Cataloguing-in-Publication Data

Weklar, Diane., 1951-
  Managing the money maze: 10 secrets to winning business financing / Diane Weklar.
    pages cm
  Includes bibliographical references.
  ISBN 978-1-933277-23-3 (trade paper) -- ISBN 978-1-933277-24-0 (kindle)
  1. Financing. 2. Business management. 3. Strategic planning. I. Title.
  HD58.8.S87 2014
  658.4'06--dc23

                              2013049701

# Dedication

To Edward J. Weklar III, who is my angel in *every* sense of the word. You make me better than I ever thought I could be.

*Mastering the Money Maze*

# Acknowledgements

The African proverb "It takes a village to raise a child" is also true in the development of a book and I want to thank my village for all their help and support. The individuals and organizations mentioned in the book deserve thanks, whether I was in direct contact or on their websites to obtain useful information.

I definitely want to thank my editor, Carol J. Amato, who read every word many times and offered suggestions and revisions, and her magic made sure that you, the reader, can easily understand all the information provided.

Special thanks go to Sophia Brooks and her CEO Collaborative. Each member of the group has provided great insight and feedback as I struggled with the content that should be included in this publication. I also want to thank Dian Wyman, CPA extraordinaire, and Janise Graham, the insurance guru, who provided great direction to the essentials that entrepreneurs need to be successful. Thanks also go to my friends at the Business Resource Connection, who are always willing to share their business expertise.

I am most appreciative of all the help I received from my book coach, Ann McIndoo, who kept me on track and focused on completing the writing of my book in a timely manner. And to Denise Cassino, who taught me all the tips and techniques that make a bestseller campaign a reality.

I especially want to thank Evan MacQueen, who shared his network of people with hands-on, up-to-date information about dealing with funding issues. I thank all the people who allowed me to interview them, but especially, Noah Glass, Steven Kaplan, Joseph Burkhart, and Mark McGovern.

My gratitude extends to Kara R. Wagner, my friend and great sounding board, who helped me clarify my thoughts. Thank you for "doing" for me.

I most grateful to Edward J. Weklar III for all the assistance and support he provided throughout the entire book process. Without his help, this book would not exist. I thank him for the countless hours of discussion, revision and positive support. This book is his as much as it is mine.

# Table of Contents

## Chapter 7 – Relationships Get You to Your Goal Faster, Cont'd.

## Chapter 8 – *Secret #1*
## Show You Are the "A" Team     99

## Chapter 9 – *Secret #2*
## The Purpose of Your Request: Show How Your Success Will Make Them Money     113

## Chapter 9 – *Secret #2*, Cont'd.

## Chapter 10 – *Secret #3*
## Know Industry Trends and Your Business Opportunities　　　　129

## Chapter 11 – *Secret #4*
## Eliminate Concentration and Increase Your Probability of Success　　　　141

## Chapter 12 – *Secret #5*
## An Effective Dashboard Will Help Navigate You to Financing　　　　159

## Chapter 12 – *Secret #5*, Cont'd.

## Chapter 13 – *Secret #6*
## Increased Profitability Can Be a Positive or a Negative     169

## Chapter 14 – *Secret #7*
## Higher Barriers to Entry Means Lower Barriers to Financing     187

## Chapter 15 – *Secret #8*
## Succession Strategies: Preparing for Disaster Can Help You Win Financing     199

## Chapter 15 – *Secret #8*, Cont'd.

## Chapter 16 – *Secret #9*
## Maximize Your Credit Score to Capitalize Your Ability to Win Financing     213

## Chapter 17 – *Secret #10*
## Personal Guarantees and Collateral     233

## Chapter 18 – Getting It All Together     245

## Chapter 18 – Getting It All Together, Cont'd.

## Chapter 19 - Alternative Financing Options 263

## Appendix A – Customer and Business Market Segmentation 269

## Appendix B – Financial and Marketing Ratios 275

# Introduction

*"Accept the challenges, so you may feel
the exhilaration of victory."*

~ George S. Patton

It takes money to start and grow a business. I wrote *Mastering the Money Maze* to provide a solution to the problem that many business leaders are facing— a lack of available financing and investment to grow their companies.

Money is almost always in short supply for small and mid-sized businesses (SMBs), which are the engines of economic and job growth in the United States. While large corporations seem to have significant stockpiles of excess cash on hand, SMBs often struggle to secure the capital they need to grow.

As a staunch supporter of SMBs, my goal is to provide you with an easy to navigate roadmap to overcome the primary obstacle of business growth—where to find business financing and, most importantly, *how to get it*!

I am always asked, "What do lenders and investors really want?" The quick and easy answer is that they want well-run companies that are poised for growth. Growth requires resources—people, technology, time, and of course, money!

Helping businesses grow has always been the guiding light of my career—whether I was in a corporate position, as a consultant helping businesses overcome challenges, or starting my own businesses.

As a business builder, I know that driving growth and increased profitability means more than creating new marketing strategies or hiring more sales people. I learned from my clients' failures, as well as my own, that a true action plan for accelerating growth requires looking at the full depth and breadth of the organization.

We must ensure that all aspects of the entity and its people are synchronized in working towards the same goals to reach a successful result. And that is what financing sources are looking for in the companies that they are considering investing in.

*Mastering the Money Maze* gives you the information to help you get financing you need from lenders and investors, and also provides you with the best practices to build a superior firm by sharing the 10 secrets to winning business financing.

## What are the Issues?

As mentioned, financing sources want to fund well-run businesses. While that seems obvious, the issue is perspective. Many times financing sources and SMBs have very differing views of what that means.

I wrote this book to provide you with an understanding of the important issues from the perspective of lenders and investors. The bonus to you is that it also provides your business with the best practices to build a superior firm.

Through my 25 years of working with both large and small companies, I have seen many trends in business—some good and some bad. But the worst is a level of misinformation, especially in the arena of securing business financing. One of the most prevalent is that if you create a "great" business plan, you can get the capital you need. But what makes a great business plan? That seems to be one of the well-kept secrets.

With this book, I will be sharing the top 10 secrets to winning business financing that lenders and investors REALLY want you to know. I will also provide you with a number of "bonus" topics that will put you light years ahead of your competition. My goal is to help you accelerate your company's growth so we can turn this slow growing economy into a growth engine for everyone.

The first step in this process is to provide clarity to all sides of the financing process. Over the years I have constantly heard SMBs state, "Banks only lend to businesses that don't need it," or that the investors "don't understand what I bring to the marketplace." These business owners are very willing to share their heart-breaking stories of how they are constantly being turned down or turned away by potential financing sources and are unable to grow their businesses.

But when we dug deeper, I saw that many SMBs did not have a strong understanding of what financing sources required and, therefore, were not adequately prepared to approach a lender or investor.

Lenders and investors were also frustrated. They commented on business executives whom they viewed as "unprepared" and proposals and presentations they viewed as "inadequate." A significant number of the proposals that financing sources received did not meet even their minimum thresholds. They were forced to decline most requests, regardless of how interested they may have been. These sources shared incidents in which the business owner just printed out their Quick-Books® reports and added their internal business plan, many with forecasts that had no research data to support their assumptions and projections.

Few lenders or investors will take the necessary time to be helpful to certain business owners to assist them over all of the hurdles. There is much more demand for money than there is supply of money available to invest, and most investors find it easier to pass and move on to the next opportunity.

Both financing sources and businesses pointed to the recent past where an individual or business had an easier time getting a loan or a line of credit or finding investment funds. Many people still have not come to terms with the fact that the economic "bubble time" of the 2000s was an outlier that we mistook for normal. We now have to understand that the requirements have changed and we need to change along with them.

Today, we live with uncertainty in almost all areas of our business lives, including the economy, taxes, asset values, regulations, and interest rates. This has created high hurdles to overcome both for financing sources and for business and these impediments must be resolved in any presentation.

Our challenging business environment is focusing us on new issues:

- The old business fundamentals have changed in the new economy.

- Disruptive technology changes are coming faster than ever.

- Productivity at all levels is essential for survival.

- Growth requires investment that is getting harder to find.

We now live in a new economy with different rules that require uncommon approaches. This is most obvious in the world of funding and lending. As business owners, you need to fully comprehend the needs of financing sources and fill those needs – just as you do with your own customers.

## Dispelling the Myths

To be successful, we must focus on the real issues, not stereotypical views or symptoms of the problem.

Below are a few of the most common myths that I uncovered during my research:

### Myth #1
*Large corporations and wealthy individuals are America's job creators; we should develop policies to support them.*

**Truth:**
In fact, the major job creators in the American economy are small businesses, yet they receive the least amount of support from financial and governmental institutions. Note these statistics from the Kauffman Foundation[1]:

- New businesses that are less than five years old accounted for all net job growth in the U.S.

- These new firms have generated approximately three million new jobs annually since 1977.

- While only half of all new firms survive to year five, 80 percent of the jobs created by those firms survive for five or more years.

New business creation has been declining since 2007, reached a low in 2009, remained flat in 2010 and declined 5.9 percent in 2011.[2] External debt markets (e.g., lenders) are increasingly important to start-up and new business, but financial institutions have tightened requirements, and the amounts provided to small business have declined precipitously since 2007.[3]

### Myth #2
*Most new companies are created by the younger generation and, therefore, we should focus on making funds available to them.*

**Truth:**
The highest rate of entrepreneurial activity belongs to the 55 to 64 age group. Over the past decade, this group has been responsible for 21 percent of business forma-tion while the 20 to 34 age bracket had the lowest.[4]

Even more interesting, according to census data, those 65 years old and over had a total of self-employment rate of 27 percent, while a comparable figure for those 25-34 years of age is 7.2 percent.[5] We tend to think of tech start-ups as being created by the young; however, among American-born founders, those older than age 50 numbered more than twice as many as those younger than 25, according to a new study from the Kauffman Foundation.[6]

## Myth #3
*New businesses are created by the well-educated.*

**Truth:**
According to the Kauffman Index of Entrepreneurial Activity,[7] the entrepreneurial activity rate among the least-educated group, which are high-school dropouts, remains significantly higher than for other educational levels. Their entrepreneurial rates started going up in 2006 and have been elevated ever since, though there was a slight decline in 2011. This demographic has the least job security, so it is likely they are being forced into self-employment more that other people.

## Myth #4
*Women business owners have the same access to capital as do men business owners.*

**Truth:**
Women own 30 percent of businesses yet receive only 5 percent of equity capital each year.[8] Also, women's small business loan approval rates are 20 percent lower than those for men.[9]

There are over 10 million women-owned businesses in the United States, employing 13 million people and generating $1.1 trillion in revenue,[10] yet capital is just one area in which many women business owners have fewer resources than men. When it comes to the first-year funding needed to get a business off the ground, women received about 80 percent less capital than men did: Based on this research, women obtained $71,000 in initial financing, while men obtained $134,000.[11]

Women rely on more internal financing to start their businesses than men do because they receive much less from outside sources for start-up funding: They obtain 48 percent from outside financing while men receive 68 percent.[12] Because women rely more heavily on internal financing, their average credit scores are 40 points lower than men's. This creates a vicious cycle: Women cannot get low-cost money, so they go to alternative lenders or credit cards paying higher borrowing costs. That means less cash flow and less chance for landing a loan.

### Myth #5
*Minority entrepreneurship is at an all-time low due to the recession.*

### Truth:
Latino business-creation rate has remained at a high level relative to previous years and other demographic groups. Latinos have gone from making up about 10 percent of all new entrepreneurs in 1996 to 22.9 percent in 2011.[13] The increase seems pretty consistent over time, rather than a one-time blip.

When we look at the 15 largest metropolitan areas, Los Angeles had the highest entrepreneurial rate in 2011, which may be due to the large populations of Latinos and immigrants.

### The Solution

The answer is to provide the SMBs with the education required to understand the expectations of lenders and investors, and provide them with the tools needed to win the financing they must have to grow their businesses. With adequate funding, small businesses can create the jobs essential to get the economy growing again.

## How This Book Will Help

In working with financing sources and businesses, I feel the level of frustration. Businesses want to know what financing sources *really* want, and financing sources want more information about a business than usually is provided. In addition to a wide information gap, there is a significant difference in expectations about how the current situation and the future opportunities of a business should be presented. Each side just does not understand what the other side wants.

I saw I could fill that chasm by being the liaison and coach—to help businesses create winning presentations and get the money they need to grow.

My focus in writing this book is to help business owners and managers understand what lenders and investors really want and to assist them in developing presentations that exceed all expectations. That means going well beyond the business plan and looking at your business just as a financing source does.

*Mastering the Money Maze* helps leaders of small and mid-sized businesses:

- Identify a variety of business financing tools.

- Evaluate which financing tools are right for each company.

- Demystify the process of working successfully with lenders and investors.

- Develop a professional and persuasive presentation to lenders and investors.

- Present the attractiveness of investing in the firm using accurate facts.

- Develop a roadmap to achieving significant financial growth.

Across these pages, I provide a practical roadmap for you to build maximum equity in your business and enable you to present your company in the best manner possible to your top financing source. I will be your coach, assisting you through the maze of identifying what financing sources want and how to give it to them.

We will discuss the process of building a relationship with the appropriate financing source. This takes time and effort, which means that you begin the financing process in advance of the need. If you are in crisis, you probably will not get the money you require from a lending institution that does not know you.

A major component to winning financing is to provide a compelling story detailing why investing in your business is not only safe but also a significant growth opportunity. I provide you with the information needed to secure the appropriate financing, and the insight to build even stronger, more-profitable businesses.

Together, we will deal with the processes of providing effective financials to detailing the efficient systems implemented by your experienced management team. Also, you will learn useful and effective processes to provide successful, exciting presentations that reflect the expanded expectations that this new economy now requires. Just as a corporation plans years in advance to go public, small and mid-sized businesses need to prepare themselves before approaching any lender or investor. This cannot be accomplished overnight.

In addition, this book will help you navigate the new and more stringent policies that financing sources have instituted. By understanding the new realities and creating the processes necessary, you will get the money you need and have it in place before you need it.

Even the most successful, accomplished business leaders can feel lost, helpless, or fearful when they are stuck in the unknown or facing a challenge in which they have a lack of information. My goal is to provide helpful guidance for business leaders to evaluate, select, and win the best financing for their companies, and in the process, identify the opportunities to grow their businesses and maximize their equity value.

I want to help you win!

# Chapter 1

# Creating a Money Mindset

*"The best way to predict your future is to create it!"*

~ Abraham Lincoln

Being an entrepreneur is not for the faint of heart. Today's business builders are a strong, courageous, determined, and innovative lot. And they are the true job creators of the American economy. A recent Kaufman Foundation report stated that "almost all new net jobs have been created by small business," and the majority of those new jobs were generated by firms that are less than five years old.

If you have picked up this book, you are probably a business owner, part of the management team or planning to establish a business. You, almost certainly, are a person who is determined to make things happen.

I enjoy working with entrepreneurs, because when they see a challenge, their minds immediately focus on how to overcome it. And getting the money necessary to turn an idea into reality is usually the first challenge that businesses face from day one.

Establishing your Money Mindset is the most important step. That means knowing what you want for yourself, for your business and for your employees. This should also guide your decision-making on how to grow your business and—just as important—which type of financing is most appropriate.

Though you may be asking for a loan or an equity investment from a company or a person, you are the client and you have the power to choose with whom you want to work.

## Where's The Money?

In most people's minds, the magic question is, "Where is the money?" And in the United States, there are a multitude of sources. Here are some financing source statistics for you to consider:

*Lending Institutions*

- 6,096 Commercial Banks in the United States[14]

    - This includes the country's mega banks to the small community lending institutions.

- 7,000 Community Banks[15]

    - These banks include commercial banks, stock and mutual saving institutions, savings and loan institutions, thrifts, and are considered by some sources to be the primary source of lending for small business.

- 6,952 Federal and State Chartered Credit Unions[16]

    - There are a large variety of credit unions. Some credit unions only serve a specific audience (federal employees or police) while others are open to everyone. Not every credit union provides business loans.

*Investment*

- 842 Active Venture Capital (VC) firms[17]

  - In 2010, venture capital firms invested approximately $22 billion into nearly 2,749 companies. Of these, 1,001 companies received funding for the first time.

- 2,600 Private Equity (PE) Firms[18]

  - Investors and funds make investments directly into private companies or buy out publicly traded companies and take them private. With some $3 trillion in global assets, PE firms invested in 15,300 companies that employ about 8 million people.

- 318,480 Active Angel Investors[19]

  - In 2011, Angels invested $22.5 billion in 66,230 companies. Most were start-up or early stage companies.

There are myriad sources to approach, and each will be discussed in detail in a chapter in this book. But please note that many experts estimate that three to four times the amount from all sources comes from family and friends. Remember: they are the primary source of equity investment in small businesses.

## What Do Lenders and Investors REALLY Want?

This is a question that I hear from many business owners who are totally frustrated with their experiences approaching potential financing sources, lenders and/or investors—and moving through the process of getting funded. The first step is to understand the differences between lenders and investors and what their expectations are.

Banks are in the business of making loans—safe loans (*debt financing*)—that will be repaid in a timely fashion and make them money through fees, interest, and ancillary services. The granting of credit is the rule of banking.

Making *equity* investments in companies with great promise is what investors do. But investors—Angels, venture capital and private equity firms—differ from lenders in that they look to own some portion of your business and make a lot of money in exchange for their potential investment.

All financing sources understand that there is an element of risk in every loan and investment. Their strategy is to analyze the business comprehensively, to determine whether the business meets its requirements and whether investing would be a reasonable risk. They comprehensively evaluate the balance between risk and the reward.

There is a decision-making process at each lending institution and investment firm that can be lengthy and bureaucratic. There are multiple people involved in each and every financing, whether it is a debt or an equity investment. The goal in winning business financing is to prove to each person along the process that you and your business are the right company to work and grow with.

Throughout this book, we will focus on helping you make the best impression by delivering a superior presentation and proposal. Overall, both lenders and investors look for well-run companies. We will also present a variety of best practices that you can implement to improve your business and show financing sources that you are that well-run company they have been seeking.

## The Choice is Yours: Debt or Equity

The goal of creating an effective Money Mindset is to understand yourself, your business, the level of risk, and the level of partnership with a third-party with whom you are willing to live—all of which can vary widely from person to person. In terms of financing types, the initial decision is between debt and equity, or a combination of the two.

Let's outline the differences between debt and equity. *Debt financing* is money borrowed that you must pay back. This will include financial requirements, such as the payment of an origination fee, monthly interest payments, and repayment of principal according to a specified schedule.

There may also be additional terms that include certain informational and operating requirements. All these terms are open for negotiation. Debt can be a loan, line of credit, a lease, or a mortgage. This can be obtained through a bank, a non-bank lending institution, or an individual. Though a lender may charge a fee and monthly or quarterly interest, the total return that a lender is looking to make is less than the return an equity investor is seeking.

*Equity* is money exchanged for ownership in your business. It can be obtained as start-up financing or as capital for growth through Angel investors, venture capital or private-equity firms. Though an equity investment does not come with a cash interest expense and it does not need to be paid back, the equity investor is seeking a higher return than the lender and expects to make money by selling the shares at some point in the future.

There are, of course, benefits and drawbacks to all types of financing. The issue is whether the advantages outweigh the disadvantages for you and your business now and in the future. We will discuss the differences, advantages and disadvantages for all forms of financing in the upcoming chapters.

So, determining whether debt or equity is best for you is a serious decision that should be based on how you see yourself, your business and its future. It's more than just the amount of money.

## How the Financing Environment Has Changed

Being a business in an easy credit environment makes success a much easier endeavor. Unfortunately, bubbles always burst, and the financing landscape is still difficult to navigate after the 2008-2009 downturn.

What many businesses still do not appear to understand, is that the time from the early-to-mid- 2000s was really an anomaly—an outlier—in terms of lending and funding environments. The time of walking into a lender's office and showing them you have a pulse and getting credit are long gone—as are the "no doc" loans that helped burst the real estate bubble. Requirements are tighter for the banks and, therefore, for you as a business owner.

Investors also are evaluating deals more carefully. They are viewing businesses much more critically, trying to ascertain how each and every investment will create wealth.

Actually, the current financing environment probably is more akin to what business owners were experiencing in the 1980s to early 1990s. So, in fact, today's financing arena may be more like what our parents faced when growing their businesses. They understood the idea that building a relationship with the local bank(s) was a necessary step in building a business. They knew the lenders in their communities and their requirements. Just as importantly, the lenders knew them. With the advent of the Big Bank and electronic banking, that relationship-building has been forgotten.

Equity investment has declined precipitously since the heydays of the early 2000s. This includes both angel investor and venture-capital transactions. While the investment community is still looking for that "Big Idea," they are also requiring that management teams have proven track records along with a great business model.

Businesses need to accept the new normal and plan accordingly. The new normal means that you must understand the risk-return relationships on which lenders and investors focus. As stated, they seek a proper balance between risk and potential returns, so they will look at a number of factors, including:

- Historical Performance

    - How have you been able to grow the business?

    - Can you show increases in revenue, cash flow, and profitability?

- Costs within the Business

    - How well do you meet the benchmarks in your industry?

    - How much of your costs are fixed or variable?

    - Can you reduce costs quickly in the event of a downturn?

- Concentration

    - Do you have client concentration?

    - Do you have vendor concentration?

    - Do you have management concentration?

- Marketing Potential

  – What is your unique selling proposition?

  – Is it based on realistic and comprehensive research?

  – What is the size of your potential market?

- Strong Understanding and Ability to Improve the Drivers of Your Business

  – Product/Services

  – Volume/Pricing

  – Clients/Vendors

  – New Opportunities

- Developing Predictors to Determine Personal and Business Creditworthiness

  – Strong Personal Credit

  – Solid Business Credit

  – Your Investment in the Business

## Market Fundamentals Have Changed

High Uncertainty, such as the economy, taxes, regulations, interest rates, asset values, have created very stiff hurdles to overcome for both financing sources and businesses. Our business environment is challenging and constantly changing. This means each business has to understand that:

- Old Business Rules Have Changed.

  – What does that mean for my business?

- We Operate in a New Digital World Where Tech is on Steroids.

  – How do we navigate it?

- Increasing Productivity is Essential at All Levels.

  – How do we get the maximum bang for our buck?

- Growth Requires Investment.

  – How do I get the money to grow?

In this chaotic environment, both financing sources and businesses have become more risk-adverse. Everyone is looking for a sure thing.

The essential thing that financing sources are looking for are well-run businesses. Lenders and investors want companies that are building maximum equity. What is maximum equity? Equity is the value of the business and its assets *over and beyond* any liabilities relating to it. A company that is focused on *strong, effective, continuous growth* is one focused on maximizing its equity value.

If you can show financing sources that you are a company that is building maximum equity that will translate into securing money for your firm.

So what do lenders and investors really want? As previously stated, lenders want to be repaid and make money by helping your firm grow. Investors want to get wealthy from a successful equity investment in your company.

The onus is not just on businesses. Lenders also have to meet their own requirements, which include more stringent underwriting controls and increased regulatory requirements. Investors also have specific parameters that they have to meet. To understand those parameters, you must understand the differences in investor types.

Once you have decided on the type of financing your business needs and the appropriate type of financing source you want to approach, the next step is to develop the presentation.

## Treat This as the Most Important RFP Ever!

Financing sources complain that most businesses are unprepared when they present to them. Your main goal is to build a company lenders and investors want to fund and make sure that the financing sources know that you are that company. This means you need to do more than just present your business plan and print out some financials from QuickBooks®.

The first step is to treat this process like the most important Request for Presentation/Proposal (RFP) or application you have ever received, and prepare for it in the same way. This is a marketing event, and you need to be creative in the way you present. You want to highlight your strengths, but do not want to lie or hide any serious issues.

This will require that you put together an inter-disciplinary team when creating this presentation. The team should include members from accounting and finance, marketing, management, and operations to ensure all parts of the company are brought into the strategy process.

To dramatically improve your chances for success in winning business financing, you need to go beyond the business plan. The business plan is invaluable when applying for financing; however, it is not the whole picture. Your business plan is the foundation of your business; it defines your vision and mission and serves as a roadmap as you move forward. But most business plans are for internal consumption. Financing sources want and need more.

The key point is that you must be as prepared as possible. Demonstrate that your company understands all the requirements of the financing source and that you can not only meet, but exceed, those requirements. Give them your map to success and profit and make that the aim of selling your proposal to them.

## Your Presentation Should Sizzle!

Your presentation is selling in its highest form. Every section should sparkle much more substantially than a business plan designed as a planning tool. So what do I mean by this? Ensure the look and feel is professional and electrifying. Motivate the financing source to pick your presentation out of the many on his/her desk because:

- It seems more interesting and successful than the others.

- It looks professional in its use of pictures and graphics.

- Your cover letter stimulates their interest and persuades them to want to read more.

Do this by personalizing this presentation to your unique situation and the financing source's require-ments. It must be personal, using specific discussions that you have had with the financing source, and note any verbal understandings.

While we will discuss the essentials of a business plan in Chapter 5, I do want to note how important your plan's Executive Summary is to a financing source. This will be the first thing that a lender or investor will read and will determine whether they want to consider investigating your business further. Create an Executive Summary that briefly outlines the salient facts in an interesting and exciting manner.

Additionally, you want each section of your proposal to include exciting narratives and exhibits. Present your numbers from a selling standpoint, and rethink how you show the interpretation of the important numbers.

This presentation needs to be a show-stopper that highlights your strengths and business growth opportunities. The objective here is two-fold: getting the money you need and building a long-term relationship with your financing source.

## Summary

There are numerous financing sources that a business can approach, but there are distinct differences between debt financing and equity funding. Additionally each lender and investor may have different requirements and expectations. You need to understand those issues and have them responded to in your presentation before you approach a financing source.

In addition, the financing environment has changed and you need to be cognizant of the "new normal" and plan accordingly. Always keep in mind that approaching a financing source is selling in its highest form. Treat your presentation to a financing source as the most important Request for Presentation/Proposal (RFP) that you have ever prepared.

# Chapter 2

# Debt Financing and Lending Institutions

*"Remember that credit is money."*

~ Benjamin Franklin

Debt can take a variety of forms: loans, lines of credit, mortgages or leases. They can be obtained through a bank, a non-bank lending institution, or an individual. Though a lender may charge a fee and monthly or quarterly interest, the total return that a lender is looking to make is less than the return that an equity investor is seeking.

Debt financing is money borrowed that you must pay back per a specified schedule. There may be additional terms that include certain informational and operating requirements. For example, you may be required to have a set amount of money in an account at that bank. Always remember that all of these terms are open for negotiation.

As stated previously, banks are in the business of making safe loans that will be repaid in a timely fashion and make them money through fees, interest, and ancillary services. Banks are in the business of granting of credit, and they understand that there is an element of risk with every loan.

## Types of Debt Financing

There are numerous debt-financing tools available to you. Below is a list of the most common sources:

- Long-term Bank Loans

- Short-term Bank Loans

- SBA Loans

- Lines of Credit

- Leasing Versus Buying

- Inventory Financing

- Customer Financing

- Factoring Receivables

- Home-Equity Loans

- Corporate Bonds

- Letters of Credit

- Credit Cards

## Debt Financing

A usual and customary choice for most businesses is debt financing. That is why it is so important to build a relationship with your local bankers. You help build the relationship for future financing with the successful repayment of debt. In addition, you do not lose control of your business as you do with equity financing. There are, however, things to consider before applying for or accepting a loan:

- Your Credit Status

  - Can your business qualify for debt financing?

- Financial Documentation

  - Do you have accurate, audited financials that truly reflect the business for the last 3 years?

- Size of Loan

  - Can you obtain enough money to meet your needs and help you grow?

- Cash Flow

  - Can you afford to repay the debt without straining the company?

- Interest Rates and Market Conditions

  - If the market changes or interest rates rise will you be able to repay the loan?

- Business Plan

  - Is your business plan up-to-date and based on solid research data?

- Collateral

  - Do you have personal and business assets you can pledge as collateral?

- Terms and Conditions

  Can you get favorable terms?

There are advantages to debt financing. The most important is that you keep control of your business as long as you remain in compliance with the terms of the credit agreement. While certain operating requirements should not interfere with running your business, your main obligation is to pay the origination fee, the monthly or quarterly interest, and the principal of the loan. With the final payment, the relationship can end. Also, the interest is tax deductible and the debt is usually a fixed monthly expense you can plan for.

The disadvantage is that to obtain debt financing, you generally need to have an established business with an operating history. Debt requires regular monthly payments, which limits cash flow. If you have difficulty paying on a timely basis, your credit rating may be impacted. Also, most lending institutions are requiring personal guarantees and the commitment of collateral in the event you cannot repay the loan.

## The Lender Process

There is a decision-making process at each lending institution that can be lengthy and bureaucratic. There are multiple people involved in every financing. At a bank, there may be a business development person, a loan officer, a risk management office at the branch, and a head of risk management for a region or for the institution. Each of these individuals may have different motivations and different experiences that may bias them against giving you the green light to get financing.

What they all have in common is that each wants to do a great job and look good in front of their bosses. Said another way; no one wants to look stupid.

The goal in winning business financing is to prove to each person along the process that you are a great investment and that everyone will look good after the loan is made. That means that you must make the best impression, deliver a great presentation, and highlight the strengths of your business to show them you are a safe bet.

The lender's decision-making process will include:

- Do we make the loan?

- If so, how much?

- If yes, how much interest and fees are appropriate for this level of risk?

- What additional financial or operational requirements should we attach to the financing terms?

A lender may be most excited about a low risk company with great growth potential and the opportunity for long-term lending opportunities. Your job is to make the lender understand that your business is an attractive investment opportunity based on the relative amount of risk and reward.

With high levels of uncertainty in every segment of the business environment, lenders are asking for more from everyone—more documentation, more guarantees, more experience and better track records. Be prepared to give them what they need.

**Summary**

If your goal is to keep ownership and control of your business and not share profits, then debt financing may be best for you. You will need a business that can handle the debt burden and is prepared to repay the loan in a timely manner.

# Chapter 3

# Equity Funding and Investors

*"In investing, what is comfortable is rarely profitable."*

~ Robert Arnott

All investors—Angels, venture capital and private equity firms—want to make equity investments in companies with great potential. But investors expect to own a portion of your business and make a lot of money in exchange for their investments.

*Equity funding* is money exchanged for ownership in your business. It can be obtained as start-up financing or as capital for growth. Though an equity investment does not come with a cash interest expense and it does not need to be paid back—it is not "free" money as some entrepreneurs may think. The equity investor is seeking a much higher return than the lender and expects to make money by selling the shares at some point in the future.

## Types of Equity Funding

Equity has a number of tools that can be accessed for funding:

- Family and Friends

- Angel Investors

- Strategic Investors

- Strategic Partnering

- Founder Capital

- Venture Capital

- Small Business Investment Companies (SBICs)

- Employee Stock Ownership Plans (ESOPs)

## Understanding Equity Financing and Investors

The investment community is composed of Angel investors, venture capital (VC) companies, private equity (PE) firms, as well as family and friends.

Angel investors are high-net-worth people who invest in early-stage businesses. Because they are individuals, they may have much more flexibility than a company of investors. Angel investors normally invest in fields where they have experience and understand the market or technology. This places limits on how much they will invest. As all investors, Angels expect to make a significant return on their investment.

Venture Capital companies are composed of financial professionals with specific parameters that focus on specific markets or industries and, in many cases, specific geographical locations (e.g., investing only in companies located in the northeastern United States).

Venture capitalists are considered "the big leagues" in equity investing. You will need to effectively demonstrate that you can make the VC a great deal of money; they look for a 25 percent (or more!) annual return on their investment. That means you must have not only the big ideas, but also the marketing research data to support that growth.

Venture capitalists have specific parameters for each "round" they fund. Customary rounds include:

- Proving Your Concept

- Building the Business and Developing a Clear Record of Revenue Growth

- Getting Ready to Go Public

Private equity firms, with their investors, will acquire a controlling or substantial minority position in a company and then look to maximize the value of that investment. Private equity firms generally receive a return on their investments through one of the following avenues: an initial public offering (IPO), a merger or acquisition, or a recapitalization. Private equity firms normally make a longer-hold investment in an operating company in targeted industry or specific investment area where they have expertise. PE firms may take on operational roles to manage risk and achieve growth in the companies in which they invest.

In equity financing, there may be multiple people involved in reviewing your request, and the process may be lengthy and bureaucratic. Equity funders are fully aware of the risk inherent in making an investment. Just as in a lending institution, everyone wants to look good to his or her boss after the investment is made.

The goal in winning equity funding for your business is to prove to each person along the process that you are a great investment, and that he/she will make a lot of money by investing in your company.

The typical equity-funding, decision-making process includes:

- Do we invest in the company?

- How much should we invest?

- How much of an ownership stake do we require?

- What operational requirements should we attach to the terms of the financing?

An equity investor may be most excited about a company that offers significant potential gains within a specific amount of time. Your mission is to make the investor understand that your business is that attractive investment opportunity. Investors are very attuned to the segments in which they invest and, just like lenders, are asking for more documentation and management teams with superior, proven track records.

The advantages of equity is that it provides financing without incurring debt, which means there is more cash available to run the business. Cash flow can be used to grow the company instead of making interest payments or repaying principal. Equity requires that you expect to have a long-term relationship with the investors, since they are now partners in your company. Additionally, investors bring business experience and can be helpful in growing the firm.

The major consideration for those thinking about taking on equity financing is that you will gain a partner who will have a voice in how you operate the business. Many equity investors become involved in the running of the company. It may be at the board level or potentially more hands-on. Remember, their goal is to maximize the value of their investment, which means significant growth in as short a period as possible.

Investors want more than just to be paid back; they want to make a lot of money on their investment. It may be attractive to you to have a motivational partner who can help maximize the value of your company. There is always the possibility that you may not like their ideas for growing the business or their informational require-ments. Investors also want specific and continuous—

and sometimes complex—reporting of your company's operations. Additionally, investors are looking for an exit, so if you are considering equity, you have to be prepared for what you will do in the future when the new shareholder wants to sell his/her shares. That means having an exit strategy in place.

## Things to Consider

To get equity financing, you have to be willing to sell a portion of the business, and this typically cannot be undone in an easy manner. This is a really big decision and should be considered very carefully. As stated, in accepting capital, the investor obtains some control of your business and shares in the profits. If you sell too much equity in the business, you may raise the capital necessary to grow the business, but you could potentially lose control of the company if you do not hold the majority of the stock.

Just as important, you need to understand that investors will stay on only as long as they get a return on their investment. As noted previously, they want a significant return on their investment. The big benefit of having investors as part of your management team is so that they can provide additional management support and can share contacts to help build the business.

When you contemplate equity financing, there are some things to consider:

- Do you have the resources and ability to attract investors?

- Will investors pay you enough money for partial ownership to meet your needs?

- Are you willing to share control of the company?

- Are you willing to share future profits? If so, how much?

- Are you comfortable with sharing trade secrets and ideas with potential investors?

- Does your business plan meet investors' requirements?

- Can your systems meet their reporting needs?

- Are you selling your shares in the company to gain personal liquidity or is the company selling newly issued shares to raise money for growth? Or both?

## Summary

If you want to grow quickly and are comfortable with sharing control of the business and its profits, then equity financing might be best for your company. You must have the "big idea" that investors believe will provide exceptional growth and market dominance.

There are myriad sources of money for growing your business. The Angel Capital Education Foundation[20] noted in a report that approximately $22 billion of investment comes from Angel investors, state funds and venture capitalists. *But three times that amount comes from family and friends.* They are a significant source for capital and they should not be overlooked.

# Chapter 4

# Is Debt or Equity Right For You?

*"Stay committed to your decisions,
but stay flexible in your approach."*

~ Tony Robbins

Making the decision regarding debt or equity financing can be a difficult one. To help with this process, use the *Business Personality and Financing Alignment Checklist* on the next page.

This Checklist will help you to determine whether what you want for you and your business matches what a lender or investor requires. There are no right or wrong answers—it's what is right for you. By reviewing the issues that financing sources will raise, and how they fit in with your personality and needs of the business, you can determine which path is appropriate.

> **Consider the importance level of each of the "No" answers on the Checklist.**

You can take the test right now to see what feels right for you at this time. But you may want to review it again after you finish reading this book to see if you make the same choices.

## Business Personality and Financing Checklist

| Type | Issue | Yes | No | Not Sure |
|------|-------|-----|-----|----------|
| Debt | Do you have business credit history of two years or more (Dun & Bradstreet)? | | | |
| Debt | Is your business credit history a "good" or better? | | | |
| Debt | Do you have good personal credit (700+ FICO score)? | | | |
| Debt | Have you ever taken a business loan? | | | |
| Debt | Was the business loan repaid in a timely manner? | | | |
| Debt | Has your business been profitable for each of the last 1-3 years? | | | |
| Debt | Will you have the cash to repay a loan without strain on the company? | | | |
| Debt | Will you be able to repay a loan if the market changes or interest rates rise? | | | |
| Debt | Do you have personal and business assets you can risk as collateral? | | | |
| Debt | Are you willing and able to provide personal guarantees? | | | |
| Debt/ Equity | Is your business projected for increasing growth in the next year? | | | |
| Debt/ Equity | Does your business have a unique patent or intellectual property (IP)? | | | |
| Debt/ Equity | Does the patent or IP protect you from competitors? | | | |

## Business Personality and Financing Checklist, Cont'd.

| Type | Issue | Yes | No | Not Sure |
|---|---|---|---|---|
| Debt/ Equity | Do you have enough time to identify and sell financing sources? | | | |
| Debt/ Equity | Does the business maintain records, making it easy to keep financing sources constantly informed? | | | |
| Equity | Is your business projected for high growth in the next 1 to 3 years? | | | |
| Equity | Do you have to keep control of the business? | | | |
| Equity | Are you willing to share your future profits? | | | |
| Equity | Are you willing to share a minority stake in the future profits? | | | |
| Equity | Are you willing to take on partners who will share in managing the business? | | | |
| Equity | Will you be able to attract investors? | | | |
| Equity | Will investors pay enough to meet your financial needs? | | | |
| Equity | Are you comfortable in sharing trade secrets and ideas with potential investors? | | | |
| Equity | Are you willing to give up minority or majority control of the business and its profits? | | | |
| Equity | Do you have the "big idea" that investors are looking for that will provide 25+ percent growth? | | | |

## Summary

When you review the number of Yes and No answers in the *Business Personality and Financing Alignment Checklist,* what do you see? Are there significantly more Yes responses for Debt or for Equity? That should be a helpful indicator for which way you may want to proceed.

You must consider the importance level of each of the No answers, however. For example, if almost all Yes answers point to Equity, but you refuse to share any level of ownership or control of your business with a partner, you may need to re-evaluate going down the equity path.

# Chapter 5

# Business Plan Essentials

*"...if a man does not know what port he is steering for,
no wind is favorable to him."*

~ Seneca

It is ironic that at a time where we now have the best technology (such as GPS and smart phones) to find our way anywhere, most businesses do not have a business plan to find their way to success. In fact, the National Business Association[21] has reported that only 22 percent of businesses have a business plan. They also reported that 64 percent of businesses do not have a marketing plan, 70 percent do not have a management plan, and 82 percent do not have a financial plan. To quote Benjamin Franklin: "By failing to plan, you are planning to fail."

A business plan outlines your plan for success. It is a dynamic document that is always a work in progress. This flexible road map helps you identify your chosen path to success through meeting constantly changing customer and market needs.

Most entrepreneurs have their growth plans "in their heads." From my experience, whether working with client businesses or my own entrepreneurial ventures, companies with well-written business plans will be much more effective in reaching their goals.

## Why a Business Plan?

If you do not have a written business plan, how do you keep on track of your goals and objectives? And how do you know that you have reached your success targets? Additionally, how does the team you are leading know which way to run? If your team does not know the targets, are they going full-speed in the right direction? And are you providing helpful suggestions for how to help the team succeed?

A business plan should provide you with a map to your business success. It is a guide to operating your business efficiently. Most importantly, a well-developed business plan helps you to anticipate any changes in your market and develop alternative solutions to help your company take advantage of those changes. You will benefit greatly from having a written business plan. It will assist you in internal planning, and it is an essential document when approaching lenders and investors.

The business plan is only a part of your presentation and proposal to a financing source. We will be discussing the various components of that strategy throughout this book. This section will identify the components that will put you well ahead of the "ordinary" approaches that businesses are currently using.

Before discussing the secrets of winning business financing, let's examine the basics of a business plan.

### Differences of Business Plan and Business Model

Your funding source may request that you explain your business model. Steve Blank, a well-respected serial entrepreneur and noted investor, stated, "A business model describes how your company creates, delivers and captures value. A business model is designed to change rapidly to reflect what you find outside the building in talking to customers."[22]

The goal of a business model is to gather objective feedback on critical assumptions:

- Revenue Model

- Pricing

- Sales

- Marketing

- Channels

- Customers

- Product/Service Features

Your business model confirms the assumptions in your business plan. Without a well-documented plan, you cannot develop a successful business model for your firm.

You also need to be prepared to answer the question, "Have you tested that?" Steve Blank also stated, "No plan survives first contact with customers." "Unless you have tested the assumptions in your business model first, outside the building, your business plan is just creative writing."[23]

Great entrepreneurs can spot trends and identify opportunities from details in customer feedback. That is where you create value. Clearly communicate the story of how you are filling the void or better serving potential customers in your business plan and business model. Also show that your plan is backed up with accurate research data from a statistically relevant sample of potential customers.

## Essentials of a Business Plan

Business plans have standard elements, which include:

- Executive Summary

- The Company

- The Industry

- Market Analysis

- Competitor Analysis

- Marketing Strategies

- Strategic Alliances (current and potential, if applicable)

- Management Plan

- Operating Plan

- Financial Plan (historical and projected financials together can be helpful)

- Appendix

Following is a review of what is included in each portion of a business plan and the important issues will be highlighted.

When developing your business plan to present to a financing source, make it exciting, compelling, and easy to understand. If you are not a good writer, consider hiring a professional to edit and to ensure the use of motivating language. Also, make your business plan easy to navigate. For any printed copies, consider using tabs to identify each section to make it easier for the reader. Many investors and lenders like to go to specific segments before reading the full plan. The aim is to make the reader want to learn more about you and your business, to continuing reading the full document and then contacting you to learn even more.

The ***Executive Summary*** provides a snapshot of your business. Most financing sources will always read this section first, so make it exciting—similar to a preview of a blockbuster Hollywood movie. Grab the readers' attention at the very start. Sell them on the significant growth potential of your business. You want the financing source to be eager to learn more about your business.

Additionally, show a financing source that you have a top-notch management team. Most funding sources will tell you that they invest more in an "A" team than in a business plan.

A history of solid achievement and success is what will differentiate your business. If you have a management team that has extensive experience, do more than just mention it; highlight its successes. This should be done in summary form for the Executive Summary, with the detail provided in the Management Plan section.

Additional information on the topic of management teams is provided in Chapter 8, "Show You Are the "A" Team." Please review that chapter for additional advice or support on this point. Remember that the perception of a top management team can mean the difference between success and failure in winning financing.

The Executive Summary is written last. You create this section after everything else is completed. This section is short, usually about one to three pages in length. It briefly summarizes the critical portions of the business plan and should:

- List primary contact information.

- State your uniqueness in marketplace.

- Emphasize the size of the opportunity.

- Outline the advantage you have over competitors.

- Explain how revenues are generated.

- Detail your financial projections.

- Discuss the proposed repayment term for lenders or exit strategy for investors.

**The Company** section of the business plan begins with all the pertinent contact information including name, business, email and physical addresses, and telephone numbers. This is important since, many times, the cover letter can get separated from the business plan. The rule is to make it as easy as possible for the readers to be able to reach you. Other components of The Company section will include:

- Company History

- Objectives of the Business

- Mission Statement (or a statement as to why you started the company and why it exists today)

- Business Model

- Products and/or Services (detailing their distinctiveness in the market)

- Future Products or Services (in development or in the planning stages)

- Advantages You Have (e.g., intellectual property)

**The Industry** component of the business plan provides an overview of the industry or market sector in which your business is (or will be) operating. Show the funding source that you understand all the major industry trends that currently affect your particular market or that may affect you in the future.

Note the major players in the industry, and detail your company's place within that market. Address the size of the market and the estimated industry sales.

The information included in this section should be based on objective and accurate research data on both your industry and any markets you have targeted. When discussing your target markets, describe the market potential and potential customers. Do not oversell or exaggerate when forecasting the potential.

Additional information to help you develop this section is in Chapter 10, "Know Industry Trends and Your Business Opportunities."

The **Market Analysis** examines the primary target market(s) for your products and services. It is usually based on geographic locations or demographics. This section details your target market's needs, as well as how these needs are currently being met. Specifically, describe how your products and services provide a better solution than the competition.

Additional information for developing this section is in Chapter 6, "Marketing Strategies and Execution."

The **Competitive Analysis** is an investigation of your direct and indirect competitors. Your assessment should state their competitive advantage and provide an analysis of how you will overcome any entry barriers to your chosen market. Additional information to help you develop this section can be found in Chapter 14, "Higher Barriers to Entry Means Lower Barriers to Financing."

Your **Marketing Strategies** section is a detailed explanation of the benefits your products and services provide and how they will be messaged to your target markets. This section also includes your sales strategy, pricing plan and distribution program. If you have a sales force, state whether they are employees on salary or commission or if they are outside representatives. Also, describe what channels you are focusing on and why they were selected.

In addition, describe your proposed advertising, social media, and promotional activities. Detail how and where you advertise, which trade shows you attend, your use of direct mail and email, infomercials, telemarketers, etc. Show financing sources how these various methodologies have improved growth, and how your future strategies will enhance that advancement. Additional information to help you develop this section can be found in Chapter 6, "Marketing Strategies and Execution."

If you have developed or identified potential opportunities for **Strategic Alliances,** detail them. Describe current, previous, and/or planned alliances with any businesses or individuals and how they will increase the visibility, revenues, as well as products and/or services of the company.

> ➢ **64% of businesses do not have a marketing plan**
>
> ➢ **70% do not have a management plan**
>
> ➢ **82% do not have a financial plan**

The **Management Plan** outlines the organizational structure of the business and provides biographies of the company's management. In this section, tout the skills and experience of each member of the management team. This management team will make or break the business; therefore, it is important to highlight their individual successes.

Additionally, describe key staff and any external resources that you have incorporated, such as your CPA, attorney, and IT consultants. If you have an Advisory Committee or a Board of Directors, provide that detail.

If you are approaching a financing source for funds to expand the business team, you must list your human resources needs and detail what positions need to be added. Also, list the timeline for recruitment for these positions. Additional information to help you develop this section can be found in Chapter 8, "Show You Are the "A" Team.

Your **Operating Plan** describes the facilities where your products and services are produced. Provide your business's physical location and describe the company's facilities and equipment.

Provide a list of your suppliers and vendors and explain why you selected them. If you have any concerns about sharing the names of essential suppliers, do not provide the specific names of the companies; instead, use a different label, such as "Supplier #1," "Supplier #2," "Supplier #3," etc.

Also list any appropriate operating details, such as a description of the manufacturing process. Describe whether you manufacture your products domestically or abroad or if production is contracted out. If there are details that you view as trade secrets, do not list the specific detail, but summarize the information you feel comfortable providing. If the financing source shows interest, your contact can follow up and you can inform him/her of the importance of keeping such information limited to a small group.

Information such as inventory needs or additional equipment and staff should be described, as well as how these additions will enhance the firm's growth and profitability.

The **Financial Plan** includes a description of your funding requirements. List your financial needs, interest rate and time frame requested if approaching a lender. If you are looking for an investment in the company, list your financial needs and the amount of equity being offered for this investment. Detail the reason you are seeking debt or equity financing and the expectations for the business over the next 3-5 years. Financing sources are interested in how quickly they will see a repayment of a loan or a return on their equity investment.

You also must provide detailed financial statements that provide a historical overview and forecasts. The financial analysis should include:

- Monthly detail for the last 3 to 5 years (or the historical detail that you have available), which will include an Income Statement, Balance Sheet, and Cash Flow Statement.

- Annual projections for next 5 years, which will include an Income Statement, Balance Sheet, and Cash Flow Statement.

- Lender repayment schedules or investor exit-strategy details.

- Possible future financing needs.

If your lender requires **Collateral**, list the assets you are pledging to secure the loan. Detail each item, list the date of purchase and initial value, as well as the current market value. Provide appropriate detail of any debt attached to a specific asset that you are pledging. If you have had the assets appraised, be sure to provide the appraisal information. For additional information to help you develop this section, see Chapter 17, "Personal Guarantees and Collateral."

Honestly discuss **Risk Issues.** Awareness of risk is a sign of a sophisticated management team and is expected by funding sources. Outline how you plan to deal with market and/or customer changes that will affect the business. Mitigating potential risks is helpful to both your plans and the financial source. While there are many risks out there, the goal is to identify how you can minimize them and be successful in all scenarios.

The ***Appendix*** to your business plan can include a variety of items and adds richness and details to your plan. These items can include:

- Research Reports

    - Summaries of pertinent data impacting marketing strategies

    - Additional information establishing credibility of your business idea

- Articles of Interest

    - Industry analysis

    - Economic indicators

    - Competitive reviews

- Product and Service Materials

    - Spec sheets

    - Photographs

- Promotional Materials

    - Branding programs

    - Marketing and sales collaterals

    - Customer testimonials

    - Investor references

- Contracts or Other Legal Agreements Pertinent to Your Business

  - Customer contracts

  - Supplier agreements

  - Lease agreements

The point should be reiterated that if there is anything that you believe is too valuable to disclose, such as a trade secret or a valuable contract, do not provide the specific detail in your business plan. Provide a summary of the information then follow up separately with additional information for those financing sources that want to learn more.

## What Financing Sources Want to See

Funding sources are looking for an integration of a business model within the essentials of a business plan. As we stated previously, they want to see that your business model actually confirms the assumptions in the business plan. Your business plan must establish that you have a sustainable competitive advantage which is backed up through comprehensive research.

The most frequent complaint among financing sources is that the business plan does not clearly explain both the opportunities and risks. After the lack of clarity, most complaints center on entrepreneurs who provide unrealistic or "hockey stick" projections supported by weak assumptions. They state that the assumptions are not supported by economic realities of the marketplace or may be too simplistic.

Additionally, financing sources find that many businesses are not aware of the full breadth of their competition in the marketplace and incorrectly state that their products and services are unique, or that there is no competition in their marketplace. Many financing sources get concerned and question whether the management team was not aware of its own market or if inaccurate information was knowingly provided. This is another reason why is it so important to conduct market research before finalizing the presentation to financing sources.

It is not advantageous to provide filtered information to a financing source. Do not omit a thorough competitive analysis or any information that may detract from your business model. If you have such information and you believe it is incorrect, you may want to provide the information with your commentary on why it is wrong and why a significant opportunity still exists. Funding sources are sophisticated professionals; omissions and mistakes do not generate a high degree of confidence and can actually cause a decline to your request.

**Success Factor Checklist**

When developing your business plan, make sure that you include the following issues, if appropriate for your business and the financing source you are approaching. Show that you have:

- An established, identifiable market segment.

- Identified a real need that your product or service fills.

- Slow product obsolescence – your product is not a fad, not perishable, and avoids high rates of technological disruption.

- Repeat buyers of your product that result in a continuing revenue stream.

- Customer contracts and/or deposits.

- Limited entrenched direct competition—ensure you are not going head-to-head with major competitors.

- Developed distribution channels to sell your products and services.

- Dependable supplies of materials, labor, and other inputs.

- Good supplier trade terms.

- Reliable production process.

- High margins that cover operating costs and provides profit.

- Strong cash flow.

- Limited product liability (or insurance), so that any potential product mistakes will not bankrupt the company.

- Intellectual property protected with patents and trademarks in the markets targeted.

- Exit potential or debt repayment strategy.

- Show that the industry is not highly regulated and will not face government interference. Or, if it is, how your management team can operate successfully and profitably in such an environment.

- Appropriate investment needs for your industry.

## Summary

Your business plan is a key piece in your presentation to a financing source. These professionals have seen hundreds, if not thousands of business plans. Make sure that yours is comprehensive and meets all the requirements of the funding source. And definitely make it sizzle—you want them to be excited about talking with you to get more information!

# Chapter 6

# Marketing Strategies and Execution

*"The purpose of a business is to create and keep customers at a profit."*

~ Peter Drucker

L enders and investors want to know how you will generate revenue for the business. That means they will focus on your marketing plan and how well you have been executing.

Marketing is a process, not an event. And marketing is more than just advertising or sales. An effective marketing plan involves setting clear marketing goals and implementing a series of marketing strategies to achieve them. Just placing a few ads is never going to draw the kind of business you need to be successful.

Too many small businesses get hung up on the cost factor of marketing. The first question always asked about any marketing strategy is, "How much does that cost?" While the cost factor is important to the overall plan, this is entirely the wrong question to ask. The right questions are, *"Will that target the right market?"* and *"What is my rate of return on that marketing spend?"*

So many companies waste resources on ineffective marketing programs because they have not spent the time to develop a coherent one that targets the right markets and customers. Without that knowledge, they do not understand what channels and strategies would be most effective to reach their ideal buyers. Instead, many businesses just "do a little bit of everything" and don't see successful results. Then they complain that marketing is a waste of money.

The key issue is that effective marketing is targeted marketing.

## Targeted Marketing

Not everyone wants or needs your products and services, so dump the idea that everyone is interested in what you have to sell, because they are not! The reality is, only the people who feel they have a need for your products and services will be interested in buying them. Effective marketing is identifying who these people are and focusing your efforts on them.

The first step is to define your target market and that means research. An effective marketing program is based on a thorough examination of the market(s) of potential customers for your products and services.

Once you truly understand your ideal markets and customers, you can select and implement effective strategies to reach them. By focusing on your target markets, you can avoid wasting time and money on ineffective programs.

Just as important, financing sources will be asking you several important questions:

- What are your target markets?

- Who are your customers?

- Why have you selected them?

- What are the growth opportunities?

- What are your future markets?

These are normal and customary questions to which you must have answers that are based in fact (your research) and not just intuition.

Mark McGovern, CEO of MobileSystem 7, is a former investor and current entrepreneur who has obtained significant venture capital for his start-up. He stated that it is very different on the entrepreneurial side of the funding process: "You must be ready to answer the hard questions, the most important being, "What are you bringing to the market?" and "Who will be buying it and why?" Just as important is what makes you better or different and who else is already in the marketplace. And the most important question that investors want you to answer truthfully is, 'What are the risks'?"

## Research is Key

The way to identify your ideal markets and customers is through research. There are numerous ways to conduct research and get the information you need. You can hire a researcher or get an intern from your local college. Or you can educate yourself by going online, taking a class, getting some books on marketing, or going to your local librarian and asking for help.

The objective is to conduct a "Marketing Analysis"—a thorough examination of your potential markets to identify your ideal customers. The first step is to define your Target Market by ascertaining who has a want or need of your products or services. The next steps are to define how large your target market is, how the people or businesses in that target market behave, where to find them, and what the best channels are to reach them effectively.

Also answer specific questions directly related to your products and services: who would use them, are there similar products on the market, who buys them and why?

# Customer Segmentation

The goal of customer segmentation is to group potential buyers into meaningful segments so you can answer the following questions:

- Is this segment worth pursuing?

- Is it possible?

- Will it be profitable?

Before starting a customer segmentation, be aware that consumer and business segments are carved out in different ways.

## Consumer Segmentation Focus (B2C)

Consumer Segmentation can be expressed as "Business to Consumer" or B2C. This is typically grouped in four broad areas:

1) Geographic

2) Demographic

3) Psychographic

4) Behavioral

This translates into detailed information about the buyers in your target market:

- How old are they?

- What gender?

- Where do they live?

- What is their family structure (number of children, extended family, etc.)?

- What is their income?

- What do they do for a living?

- What is their lifestyle like?

- How do they like to spend their spare time?

- What motivates them?

- What is the size of your target market?

You can also zero in on consumer segmentation by using 'psychographics' as your guide:

- *Lifestyle*: conservative, exciting, trendy, economical

- *Social class*: lower, middle, upper

- *Opinion*: easily led or opinionated

- *Activities and interests*: sports, physical fitness, shopping, books

- *Attitudes and beliefs*: environmentalist, security conscious

## Business Segmentation Focus (B2B)

"Business to Business" (B2B) segmentation will identify industry segments in a specific geographical area and will include:

- Companies in Each Segment

- Number of Employees

- Annual Sales Volume

- Location

- Company Stability

- How Customers Purchase (seasonally, locally, only in volume)

- Who Makes the Decisions?

Businesses typically buy products and services for three main reasons: to increase revenue, maintain the status quo, or decrease expenses. If you fill one or more of these corporate needs, you may have found a target market.

Appendix A has several charts that describe the segmentation process in detail for both consumer and business segments.

An interesting example, noted in the chart below, shows both business and consumer segmentation for Apple®[24] with its various computers, which are products that can be sold to both segments. Apple® targets its lines of Mac® computers at specific market segments. The table suggests the market segmentation that Apple® used in developing their marketing plans for the products they had in 2011.

| Markets | | Computer Products | | | | |
|---------|---------|------------|--------------|------|-----------------|-------------|
| Sector | Segment | Mac Pro | MacBook Pro | iMac | MacBook Air | Mac Mini |
| Consumer | Individuals | ✓ | ✓ | ✓ | ✓ | ✓ |
| | Small/Home Office | | ✓ | ✓ | ✓ | |
| | Students | | | ✓ | ✓ | ✓ |
| | Teachers | | ✓ | ✓ | | |

| Sector | Segment | Mac Pro | MacBook Pro | iMac | MacBook Air | Mac Mini |
|---|---|---|---|---|---|---|
| Professional | Medium/Small Business | ✓ | ✓ | ✓ | ✓ | |
| | Creative | ✓ | ✓ | ✓ | | |
| | College Faculty | | ✓ | ✓ | ✓ | |
| | College Staff | | | ✓ | | ✓ |

## Marketing Channels

As you segment your customer base, the additional questions that should be asked include how do they access information (e.g., read newspapers/magazines, watch television, web surf) and where do they hang out (e.g., trade conferences, shopping malls, gyms)?

Be where your targets are if you want to grab their attention. Each of these channels may demand a different market strategy and needs to be coordinated if implementing an integrated marketing approach.

## Competitive Analysis

Gather information about your competition (both direct and indirect) that can impact your company:

- Who are your competitors?

- Who are the major players?

- What makes them the leaders?

Review the products and services they offer and how they differ from your offerings. Additionally, look at their branding, marketing strategies and channels.

Financing sources will always ask for current and projected information about your target market, which may include:

- What proportion of your target has used a similar product or service?

- How much of your product/service might your target buy? (Estimate this in gross sales or units sold)

- What proportion might be repeat customers?

- How might your target market be affected by:
  - Demographic shifts
  - Economic events
  - Larger socioeconomic trends
  - Government policies
  - New regulations or changes in taxes

## Marketing Research Sources

There are myriad market research sources you can use to obtain this information, both online and offline, such as:

*Online Sources*

- American Marketing Association—www.MarketingPower.com

- American Society for Association Executives—www.ASAECenter.org

- FreeDemographics.com

- Google (a great starting point for any question)

- Mashable.com (social media stats)

- SBTDC.org (good starting place for research sources)

- U.S. Census—www.census.gov

*Offline Sources*

- Board of Trade

- Chamber of Commerce

- City Hall

- Economic Development Agencies

- Local Libraries

Once you have compiled this data and analyzed it, you will have a clear definition to whom you are selling, what their needs are, and how you can differentiate your company from the competition.

## Unique Selling Proposition

You have to be able to answer the question, "Why should I buy your product or service?" This is accomplished by creating a unique selling proposition (USP), which sets you apart from the competition.

Most well-known, successful companies have USPs:

- Apple — Think Different

- Allstate — You are in good hands with Allstate

- BOSE — Better sound through research

- BMW — The ultimate driving machine

- Energizer Batteries—It keeps going, and going, and going...

63

These are the types of businesses that quickly draw you in (or repel you if it is not done well), because of who they are. They communicate their uniqueness, and it's clear from the first minute you come into contact with them, you know what they're all about.

Notice that only a few companies have invented entirely new topics or products. Each business sells something people already buy (computers, cars, insurance, electronics), but they have each taken a unique approach that gives them a significant advantage over other players in their respective markets.

A Unique Selling Proposition enables you to compete directly in a crowded space of competitors. Instead, your company will stand out for its distinctiveness and make building a big audience so much easier.

Get creative as you develop your USP. A good example is TOMS Shoes. There are numerous outlets for buying shoes, and while they offer shoes that are quirky and inexpensive, that is not enough to stand out in the crowded shoe business. The unique and compelling part of the TOMS Shoes story is that they give a new pair of shoes to a child in need for every pair you purchase.

Another example is Kiva, who in 2005 launched and brought microloans online. While there are many places that loan money for profit and many more to donate money to help change people's lives, Kiva loans money to change lives. Kiva has loaned over $450 million to small entrepreneurs in the world's poorest places with a repayment rate of 99 percent! A very unique and compelling USP.

Your research should help you design a USP that will boost your sales and profits by positioning yourself as the best choice in the marketplace:

- Describe what you do.

- Communicate the solution you provide.

- Show how you differ from the competition.

- Explain the value you bring to your market.

Don't develop a Marketing Plan without one! Your financing sources will be looking for it in your presentation and your business plan.

## Promotional Activities

Now that you have defined your target market and segmented your buyers, focus your promotional efforts on your ideal clients and no one else. But it can be difficult to create promotional programs without really defining to whom you are speaking.

The easiest way to do that is to create a model of your ideal customer or, in marketing lingo, an "Avatar." This is a fictional representation of the type of person you are targeting. This can help you in speaking directly to your ideal client and creating effective marketing strategies to reach your target audience. You can obtain this information for your specific business from the research statistics taken from your market analysis.

For example, for a client with a retail store selling lingerie, a marketing analysis was conducted and her Avatar identified as: Mary, 30 years old, working professional, married with one young child. Mary does not read newspapers at all, but gets most of her information off the Internet or her smart phone. She spends increasing time emailing, texting, and on her Facebook and Twitter accounts. Occasionally, Mary picks up a glossy women's magazine when she's going through the grocery checkout.

Our research identified where Mary spends her "non-work" time: taking her young daughter to preschool and a local park with a playground. She is very physically active; she takes yoga and goes regularly to the gym.

Mary and her husband do seasonal sports: biking, skiing and snowboarding. Mary's hobby is cooking, and she likes to try out gourmet recipes now and again. She is in her car a lot but listens to preprogrammed music.

We then compared the business's current marketing activities with her Avatar and found that the retail store used a Yellow Page ad, several different newspaper ads, and radio promotions on holidays like Valentine's Day. This showed us that the business's current marketing strategies were ineffective for the person that they were trying to reach. They were, in fact, wasting money on ineffectual programs.

This illustrates that you need to select marketing strategies that would be most likely to reach your target market Avatar and implement them. In this case, a website and Facebook page and banners on websites focused on young children, exercise or cooking would be more appropriate.

## Positioning

Positioning is a marketing concept that outlines what a business should do to market its product or service. When positioning, you create an image for the product based on its intended audience; for example, premium or commodity. This is created through using the four "Ps" of marketing: product, price, place, and promotion. The more directed the positioning strategy is to your target audience, the more effective the marketing strategy is for a company. Also, a good positioning strategy elevates the marketing efforts and helps a buyer move from product or service knowledge all the way through its purchase.

Understanding your target customers and your competitors assists you in successfully positioning your products and services. With this information, you can delineate your prospects' decision-making criteria and hot buttons that drive the initial interest (usually emotionally based) and what you specifically do that is unique or better.

For example, if competitors have a distinct weakness, a winning Positioning Strategy may be to highlight your strengths in areas where your competition is weak. If your company is re-defining the rules of the game or introducing a new way of doing things, this may place you in the industry leadership or visionary position.

> **Your positioning strategy should answer the question, "Why should I buy your product or service?"**

It's very important to have a winning positioning strategy. If you cannot clearly articulate how and why you're different, no one else is going to do it for you. The risk of not having a positioning strategy is that you may be forced to compete on price.

Always remember your competitors are trying to figure out how to become better and get a leg up. Your job, then, is to continually assess whether a particular positioning strategy is still valid and, if not, adjust it accordingly.

## Features and Benefits

Many people don't understand the difference between features and benefits, and unfortunately, this can be a huge detriment when you're writing product copy. A feature is a physical or tangible aspect of, or a factual statement about, a product or service that you are promoting. A benefit is what happens to your customers when they take your product or service and implement it. In other words, a benefit tells your customers *why* your features matter or "what's in it for them."

Common marketing strategies focus on the fact that most prospective customers tend to buy based on benefits. They are looking for solutions to the problems that they have in their lives and a benefit explains to them how your product solves those issues.

Remember that a benefit is a result of a feature. For example, if you tell your customers that you are there any time they need you, explain that you have a 24/7 customer service call center, otherwise, it sounds like a sales pitch.

An effective way to sell your products and services are *benefits verified by features.* If you list a relevant feature and then explain why that feature is important to your customer, you can bring to life the exact reasons why a customer should buy your products or services over those of your competition.

## Track and Measure Marketing Programs

Follow the performance of your marketing efforts closely. One way to do so is to be vigilant about tracking how each customer finds you. Include the question on any inquiry form on your website and ask each time a new customer comes in to your brick and mortar store, if you have one.

Track the success of each marketing campaign you conduct. Determine what aspects made it effective—or not effective—so you can improve in the future. Keep in contact with your prospects and customers and measure which types of programs bring in buyers—blog, website, contests, coupons, etc.

Do the math to figure out how much you've spent to attract that customer, and see if he or she keeps coming back. The marketing cost of attracting that customer will go down—and your profits will go up—once the customer starts spending more and more with you throughout the year.

## Marketing Budgets

Marketing is an investment, but make sure you are making a good investment. A good marketing budget should always mirror the goals of the organization—no matter how aggressive or conservative they may be.

Marketing budgets can range from one to ten percent of sales or more, depending upon a variety of factors: how established your business is, what industry you are in, and how much you can really afford.

The most realistic way to proceed is to determine the marketing program and the cost to implement it effect-tively. Determine the specific undertakings you need to employ (web development, advertising, public relations, development of marketing materials, etc.), and tally the costs. Base the budget for marketing expenditures on the total.

Use the previous years' expenditures when creating a marketing budget, but ultimately, you will need to cus-tomize a plan for growth that's the best fit for your company's short- and long-term needs. For instance, if you're a small, startup tech company, you may need to spend a higher percentage of your total operating budget on marketing and building buzz versus an established consulting firm that may already have a great market penetration and brand awareness.

If you are in the first years of your business, you should be investing as much as you possibly can. Once you become established and profitable, the percentage can drop, depending on the type of business you have and your profit margins.

Once you have your annual amount, the challenge then becomes one of allocating among the many marketing channels available to you. The key when allocating among them all is to start by thinking about exactly whom you want to reach, and what channels and media they're likely to use.

Marketing budgets will change along with the rest of the company's projections and strategic plans. Revise your marketing budget annually to ensure that the spending is realistic. Review the success of the past year's budget and apply what you learn to make future budgets more efficient. Create a budget that makes the most sense for your business at this time.

> **Many companies waste resources on ineffective marketing programs because they have not targeted the right customers.**

Even in a recession, it is wise to keep the marketing budget intact. Yet, it's often the first thing cut when times get rough. Cutting back on marketing will mean losing out on even more profits in the future.

## Summary

To establish an effective marketing program, identify your target market and understand how your ideal clients behave. Your marketing strategies should be built around the wants and needs of your target customers and designed to reach them easily through the channels they use.

Marketing does not provide instant results. *Repeated* practice gets you to your goal. Don't do everything at once; that is a recipe for failure. Once you "master" a strategy and find it to be successful, add another. Test to see what works for your customer base. Always keep good records of each strategy and program you implement. Analyze all aspects of each campaign to ensure you are always using best practices. Evaluate results of all marketing programs to ensure you are responding to the constantly changing needs of your targets.

Remember, effective marketing is targeted marketing.

# Chapter 7

# Relationships Get You to Your Goal Faster

*"Nothing is as fast as the speed of trust.*
*Nothing is as profitable as the economics of trust.*
*Nothing is as central to leadership as relationships of trust.*
*It truly is the one thing that changes everything."*

~ Stephen R. Covey

**"N**o man is an island" is especially true when building a business. Whether you want to build a legacy business that lasts forever or a quick build and exit, you will need help. Many small business owners have experienced tremendous success in many areas. Based on their history of success, many entrepreneurs believe that if something needs to be done (and done right), they must do it themselves.

While it may be true that entrepreneurial business owners are best suited for leading certain projects, it is also true that many entrepreneurs fall into the trap of being penny-wise and pound foolish. They fall victim to the belief that they have to do it all—take significant time to research, become experts in all topics, and continue to further their role as super entrepreneurs all in the name of saving money.

In fact, if you are one of these entrepreneurs, this belief not only tends to slow you down, but also may be the cause of your failure. We all know the numbers—about half of all new establishments survive five years or more and only one-third survive 10 years or more, according to the US Small Business Administration.[25] According to credit reporting agency Dun & Bradstreet, small business failures increased by 40 percent from 2007 to 2010.[26]

To be successful in the treacherous waters of business building, take advantage of experts to augment your specific areas of expertise. This means building relationships with (and buying services from) those members of the business community from whom we want to learn and with whom we want to do business. This includes experts in areas such as sales, marketing, taxation, law, procurement, manufacturing, and supply chain management. And, let's not forget our important potential partners: financing sources.

The old adage "people do business with people they know and trust" is true whether you are growing your customer base or looking for financing sources. This is the main reason to build relationships.

## What These Relationships Involve

Relationships with financing sources are unique and different from those of other business associations. Obviously, they are more intimate than the relationship you have with the vendor supplying you with services or materials. Financing sources want to know all about you—and yes, that can be frightening.

Funding sources do become privy to all the internal operations of your business, and they will frequently voice their preferences to your business practices. Depending upon the financing source, these preferences will range from one extreme of only gentle suggestions that you can ignore to the other extreme of the threat of terminating your relationship.

You need to view your business operations from the perspective of a financing source. Your funding source will assess the risk to their investment, the competence and experience of the management team, as well as the probability of repayment, if it is a lender, or the creation of wealth, if it is an investor.

Funding sources are financial professionals who have a deep understanding of specific industries. They want to work with management teams who have demonstrated historical success and provide confidence in their ability to achieve future success. Understand that financing sources have a large pool of potential companies they can finance.

In addition, they have a lot of internal regulation they need to get through in order to provide just one company with financing. Reiterating an earlier point, they want to look good in front of their bosses and to demonstrate good judgment in their internal processes. Since they have to work hard to provide you with financing, they expect a lot from you. In particular, they want to know:

- How well you articulate your particular financing needs and how that will grow the business.

  - Financing sources want more than the statement, "I need this amount of money to buy (equipment, facilities, employees, etc.)." They want to know specifically how this money will positively impact the growth of the company over the short term (one year) and long term (two to five years).

- How strongly your business has performed historically based on a variety of operating metrics, including revenue, profitability and cash flow.

- While past performance is not a guarantee of future results, many financing sources want to understand how your business has performed historically (over the last 2-3 years). If you are forecasting a significant difference in such areas as future sales, expenses, and cash flow, the financing source will be focused on how you will achieve such improvements. Specifically, state how your results will be impacted by receiving additional funding.

- How appropriate the documents are that you provide to them.

  - In addition to providing accurate, up-to-date information, you must be able to "talk the details" and show them that you are in control of every aspect of the business's operation.

- How well you can explain deviations from historical trends, budgets, and industry norms.

  - They will look at both industry trends and industry ratios, comparing you to the competition.

- What efficient systems have been implemented to ensure that the management team has timely and accurate information to drive the performance of the business.

  - This will include financial, operational and marketing systems to ensure concise reporting and forecasting. They want to see clearly that your information systems allow for the strong performance of the business and healthy returns on their investment.

- How they will benefit from investing in your company.

  - Lenders want specifics on how they will be paid in full. Investors want to know how and when you will reach their required Return on Investment (ROI).

## Build a Relationship with Your Bank

Start building banking relationships as soon as you can. The fact is that, sooner or later, you will be approaching lending institutions with a financing proposal. Cultivate a relationship with lenders *before* you request a loan.

The first step is to get to know the managers of several banks in your area. Meet and get to know the loan officers as well. With community banks, since they are generally smaller institutions, meet with the presidents and the chief lending officers. Also get to know the staffs. You never know what influence each person has within the institution or what position she/he may have in the future.

The best way to get to know bank managers and loan officers is to invite them to breakfast, lunch, golf, or to see your office and meet your staff. As part of the "getting to know you" process, find out what lending authority they have, what types of financing tools they believe might be appropriate for your business, and what examples of financing they have provided to other similar companies.

Building a relationship can start with something as simple as setting up a checking account and a savings account. It is important to visit the bank often. For example, make your deposits in person and say hello to the manager. When you are in the bank, let your contact(s) know how well your business is doing. After each new business win, for example, announce to your contact at the financing source that you won a new contract or that you are making a big deposit.

Remember, the whole reason for doing this is to build a relationship with the management of the bank that you are going to approach in the future to get financing. Opening accounts at the bank before you approach them with a proposal for getting money is important. It is much harder for a lender to say no to a customer of their institution than it is to say no to a stranger.

## Electronic Relationships Just Don't Cut It

The best and most convenient service offered by banks is electronic banking. Today, you can get your clients to send payments automatically to your bank account; you can pay all your bills online without the hassle of getting stamps or going to the post office. You will have an electronic record of when your money was deposited, the when and how much was paid on each bill. Everything you need is now at your fingertips.

The convenience of electronic banking, however, has made us strangers with the lenders in our communities. When was the last time you were even in your bank? Or do you bank at an institution that does not have brick-and-mortar locations? How do you think that impacts your relationship or lack thereof with a funding source?

What this means is that when you approach a financing source, you are just a number on a spread-sheet. And, to you, lenders are just brands, not people. Just as in any business, people like to do business with people they know and like. Does your bank know who you are? Does your bank know what your business does? Does your bank know how important your business is to the community, including to their other clients? And do financing sources know how you can help them grow?

## Shop for the Right Lender

Determine which lending institution would be the most helpful to you. It might be easier to get financing, a line of credit or a loan from a local community bank than from a big bank. In the U.S., community banks are the primary source of lending for small business, according to the FDIC.

> **Cultivate a relationship with lenders before you request a loan.**

Your job is to comparison shop. Meet with a number of lending institutions to find the one that is best for you. Ask your colleagues, clients and vendors for referrals to lenders with which they have relationships. Even more importantly, have them introduce you to the bank president or the chief loan officer.

Coming in as a referral puts you in a whole different category that provides many advantages. Also, it may be beneficial for you in winning additional business from your clients, or even obtaining pricing discounts from your vendors, if they learn that you plan to expand your business based on the additional funding you expect to gain.

Many lending institutions offer educational programs and events. This is a great way for you to introduce yourself to the presenters, ask for their business cards, and set up a time to talk with them. Their job is to bring in new business, and in-person introductions are a great way to begin the relationship with a lender.

When scouting out lending institutions, speak with the branch managers as well as the lending officers about their specific lending criteria. Request a copy of their List of Requirements; this will form the basis of your presentation to them. Note that each institution will have specific requirements. Do not assume after talking to a couple of banks that all have the same needs.

At your meetings with lenders, find out about each bank's customer service programs, as well as any special terms or incentives that they may offer. Some banks offer "specials" for companies in specific market segments, or within certain geographies, industries, or even the size of the business.

Part of their job description is to support small business, and they, just like you, are always looking for new clients. Banking is a business and, just like your business, they have targeted their ideal type of customer and designed a series of products to service that target audience.

Before you begin this process, it is helpful to have a list of questions ready for them to answer. These questions include:

- What types of businesses do they target?

- Does this bank finance startup companies? (If you are a startup)

- What is the minimum number of years of historical revenue, profitability, or cash flow data that the bank requires?

- What is the minimum amount of revenue, cash flow, or profitability that a business needs to generate to be considered for a loan?

- What is the minimum loan amount provided to clients ($100,000, $50,000, $25,000)?

- Does it require a minimum credit score (personal and business)?

- What are the minimum collateral requirements?

- Does it require personal guarantees?

- Do they provide equipment or working capital loans?

- What other requirements are there for a business applying for money?

- What are the requirements for obtaining a company credit card from that bank?

Ask each lender how they determine their underwriting requirements for your type of financing. Are there particular ratios that they focus on—such as Debt Service Coverage (The cash flow available for your debt service divided by debt service itself) or Return on Assets (your assets divided by your profits). Each lender puts a different level of importance on specific financial metrics, so ask what is important to the lender. (Chapter 12 discusses financials in more detail.)

Lenders may depend highly on credit scores. They look at both personal and business. Some lenders have hybrid systems that bring in a number of factors in addition to credit scores. Find out the specific requirements and criteria of the lender that you want to approach. Some banks expect you to establish checking and savings accounts with them. Some lenders require minimum levels of cash in each account, and may even require that the cash be kept in the account for a specific length of time prior to being provided a loan or for the length of the loan term. Know what your lender expects before you apply for a loan or line of credit.

Obviously, the questions that you ask will be based on your particular situation, but it is imperative that you ask all the questions up front to make sure that you are approaching the most appropriate lender for your needs. Do not hesitate to switch to a lender that can better accommodate your lending circumstances.

Everything is negotiable—that includes interest rates and the terms of repayment. Work with your advisors, such as your CPA and your attorney, to determine the best rates and terms that you can get.

Avoid submitting a request if there is a good chance that you are not going to be approved. This is important, because lenders will find out that you were turned down when they run your credit report. If one lender identifies that your business was turned down for credit, a different lender may be more cautious (or less likely to approve) when reviewing your loan application, which is why it is important to choose the right lender for you.

Also, do not take a shotgun approach—sending your loan request to as many lenders as possible just to see if one bites. Select the best lender that will give you the greatest opportunity to get financing for your business. Again, this is not a one-shot deal. We are talking about building a long-term relationship with your potential lender. As your business grows, you will need additional financing in the future and will want multiple lenders *competing* for your business.

## What Lenders Want

Lenders want a complete understanding of your company, current situation, and plan for the future. If you present a package that leaves out details, is unclear or confusing, or provides conflicting information, your file will be red-flagged. So, it is very important for you to double check all of the facts in your presentation before you present it to a lender.

Lenders most prefer to lend to businesses that have track records of solid historical performance, including consistent annual revenue growth, profitability, and cash flow. Lenders also want to lend to companies that can demonstrate that they have the potential for continued success in the future.

While lenders are hesitant to lend to startups where there is no history of growth in revenues, they do make exceptions. Banks lend to startups that have great ideas and excellent management teams. They might have stricter credit standards for startups and may ask for more collateral and/or a personal guaranty, but there may be opportunities for you to ask for these exceptions. If the lender knows and trusts you, your proposal has a greater opportunity to get funded.

> **Lenders want to work with you over the long term, just as you want to do with your customers.**

If the financing source senses misinformation, you will face a whole host of questions, which, in turn, take up a lot more of your time and their time. This can lead to the conclusion that your request just is not worth their time and effort. Or worse—the lender may believe that you are hiding something. Again, all of these issues risk a rejection of your financing request and could possibly jeopardize your chances with other financing sources.

In almost all cases, you will be asked detailed information about your request. Be thoroughly educated in all aspects of the request to respond quickly to their questions and requests. If lenders see that you do not know the answers or continually have to check with someone else, they may think you are trying to provide only the information that lenders want to hear, rather than providing the full truth. This can be another red flag that can cause your request to be declined.

## Can Lenders Make Money Working With You?

Lenders want to be repaid; that is why they are especially interested in knowing how you make your money. They want details on the clients and customers that you serve as well as the kind of products and services you provide and how they are delivered. They also want to know how you generate your revenue and whether there are any secondary repayment sources.

Lenders collect as much information as possible to gain confidence that you are unlikely to go into default after they provide you with financing. Being generally conservative institutions, lenders want to feel confident that your business has sufficient assets and collateral to pay off the principal in the event the loan goes into default.

Most people think that banks make their money only on interest. Yes, they do, but the fees charged are even more lucrative. Their business models are based on offering their customers a bundle of services that creates revenue through interest and fees. The loan officers working with you may be compensated or judged by the origination fees they generate during the year (not the interest you are paying).

It costs seven to ten times more for most businesses to obtain a new customer than it does to maintain and up-sell a current one. Lenders are looking to work with you over the long term, just as you look at your clients and prospects for increasing revenue.

Lenders look at you as a revenue source. Interest rates are somewhat standard in the industry and are based on specific criteria, which will differ by company, so that is generally not the area in which they look to increase growth. They want to provide you with a whole host of services that will generate fees for the bank, as well as increase loan volume and the growth of their business.

## Conducting a Lender Comparison

Just as you comparison shop for every piece of equipment and software for your company, you need to shop lenders for the best rates and terms. But you also need to conduct your research in an organized fashion. First, determine the type(s) of potential financing and its purpose. For example, are you shopping for short-term debt for building seasonal inventory or long-term debt to purchase a facility?

### Create a Lender Questionnaire Worksheet

There are specific questions to ask each lender you approach. You need make sure that you ask each lender the same questions. These questions will be customized based on your specific situation and your needs. Additionally, you should record the answers that each lending institution supplies, so you can compare what each lender is providing. If you don't understand what they want, always ask for clarification.

On the next page is a sample Lender Questionnaire Worksheet.

## Lender Questionnaire Worksheet

Name of Lender_____

Date_____

Contact_____

Position_____

Telephone_____Email_____

Address_____

| Question | Comment | Notes |
|---|---|---|
| Do they fund businesses in your industry? | | |
| Do they fund businesses in your specific sector? | | |
| If so, what other companies in your industry have they funded? | | |
| At what stage of business development do they provide financing? | | |
| On what basis do they generally provide help? | | |
| Does this lender finance startup companies? | | |
| What is the minimum loan amount they finance? | | |
| What is the minimum number of years of financial data required? | | |
| Are there minimum collateral requirements? | | |
| Do they require personal guarantees? | | |
| Do they make equipment or working capital loans? | | |

*Create a Lender Comparison Chart*

Next, do a comparison of the terms and requirements each has provided. Below is a sample Lender Comparison Chart that you can develop to simplify the lender selection process.

## Lender Comparison Chart

| Lender | Loan | Purpose | Size $ | Int Rate % | Fees $ | Payback Terms Years | Pro | Con |
|--------|------|---------|--------|------------|--------|---------------------|-----|-----|
| A | Credit Line | Inventory | 150K | 9.0 | 150 | When Used | Readily Available | High % |
| B | Real Estate | New Facility | 999K | 10.5 | 9,000 | 25 | Standard Terms | High % |
| C | SBA Loan | Working Capital | 350K | 8.0 | 2,200 | 5 | Guarantee | Complex Process |
| D | Lease | Equipment | 50K | 12.0 | 3,000 | 7 | 100% Financing | High Fees |

## Build Relationships with Investors

Just as you should build relationships with lenders, apply the same strategies when approaching investors. Investing is a relationship business. The investment community is a very collegial group: they know each other, work with one another and socialize together. Information regarding trends, companies, and technologies is shared. If you meet with investors who are not interested in your business, always ask if they can refer you to someone else.

Steve Kaplan, an attorney with Pillsbury Winthrop Shaw Pittman, provides legal counsel to entrepreneurial companies in the high-tech and other high-growth sectors. Based on his experience, he provided some really good tips. The most important are, "You do not want to be seen as 'stranger money.' Set up relationships so investors can actually know you in a business setting, so they see that your management team is experienced and has worked together well. Investors are betting on 'who you are' not 'what you do.'" This is another reason to create a strong rapport.

Steve explained, "This is a relationship business, since the community is small, building relationships is essential. My top tip to entrepreneurs is if you ask for money, you will get advice; if you ask for advice, you will get money. Build a reputation of integrity and honesty, because this is a multi-stage game."

As with lenders, the investment process can be long and complicated. Your contacts must justify this investment to partners, committees, and funders, so they want to look good by making good investments. Their compensation depends on these good investments, so they will be cautious. You need to "provide the story" so that they can convince the decision-makers.

Mark McGovern, CEO of MobileSystem7, and a former venture capitalist, understands both sides of the financing process. "The guy sitting across from you is not the decision maker," he says, "so you need to specifically ask 'What is your decisioning process and what does it take to get a win.'"

Mark's top tip in building a relationship is to "Be dynamic, yet humble. Listen to people and learn from each interaction. The best interactions may be with people who don't know your product. Engage them so they give you thorough feedback to ensure you clearly describe what you do."

## Understanding Investor Types

As stated previously, the main investors are Angels, Venture Capital (VC) and Private Equity (PE) firms, though family and friends are still major contributors to many early-stage companies. Note that each of these entities fund at different stages of a company's lifecycle.

Angel investors are an important source of startup and early-stage funding. While an Angel is usually a high net-worth individual who invests his/her own money, there are a growing number of Angel investing groups that work together in funding companies.

Venture Capitalists are individuals who work at professionally managed firms and invest money obtained from pension funds, insurance companies and other sources to build a portfolio of businesses. While some do early stage companies, most invest in proven ideas that need to be expanded or are getting ready to go public.

Private Equity firms make direct investments into established private companies by acquisition or divestiture or buy-out publicly traded firms and take them private.

### *Angel Investors*

Angel Investors invest early in a business lifecycle and usually fill the gap between startup and venture capital stages. It can be difficult for startups and early-stage companies to find Angels, particularly ones that have an interest in your specific business idea. There are several strategies that will enable you to get Angels on your radar. A highly effective strategy includes networking. There are a number of organizations of Angel groups all over the country. You can research them and find out if there's one near you. You can start with:

- Angel Capital Association (AngelCapitalAssociation.org)

- Gust (gust.com), the leading platform of Angel investing groups

- National Angel Capital Organization
  (http://gust.com/angel-group/national-angel-
  capital-organization)

Another strategy is to get media attention for your company so Angels can find you. If you have an exciting new idea about which the world starts buzzing, funding can come to you. Also, your internet research should provide you with lists of Angels in your local area. With this list, you can begin the process of meeting them.

Probably the best and easiest way is getting referred to an Angel. Your attorney, CPA, consultants, and other local business owners you already know, may have relationships with Angel investors. Ask them to help you traverse the maze and get you in front of an Angel investor. Additionally, there are Internet matching services that may be appropriate for you.

In addition, you can expand the concept of who is an Angel: successful business owners, real estate developers, and serial entrepreneurs may be good candidates. Noah Glass, Founder and CEO of OLO, which provides online ordering for fast-growing restaurants, found his Angel investor from a non-profit board on which they both served. He noted, "I approached him with my prototype, and asked for advice. Since we had a working relationship from the work we did on the Board, I was a known quantity. After discussing my plan, he provided significant startup funding. Everything flowed from creating a network."

Steve Kaplan states, "Today you see a number of Angels providing $25,000 checks to a company, rather than a lead investor providing $250,000, so you end up with a Cartel of Angels. In fact, a big issue today is what I call Angel wrangling, where you bring a number of angels together to discuss how they all can invest in the same company. If that is not handled effectively, it can have a very bad result."

The Angel investing process is an organic process that can be looked at in a two-step strategy: 1) talk with everyone and get soft interest; and 2) qualify each lead and determine the best way to get the deal done with a small number of investors. Work with your legal as well as financial advisors as you develop these strategies.

### What Angels Want

Angel investors are not venture-capital firms and do not operate in the same manner. While they may not require as much due diligence as a venture-capital firm will expect, they do require a strong, solid business plan, good financials and realistic projections. Please note, they will read your proposal and business plan in detail. Their main focus is to find a company that will make them money.

Most Angels have specific areas of specialization and do not operate outside of those parameters. They usually invest in companies where they have experience and knowledge. Their focus may be a specific industry group, a particular market segment, and a certain geographical area. The investment size that these investors provide may vary widely from Angel to Angel.

Some Angels may expect to provide advice infrequently and be passive investors, but many expect to take a more active role in helping you grow or manage your company. You may greatly appreciate the advice of certain Angels, or you may not like the advice provided. This is why you need to get to know the Angels. You want to have a great relationship with the individuals who invest in your business.

### Venture Capital and Private Equity

While Angels manage their own money, Venture Capitalists (VCs) and Private Equity (PE) firms manage other people's money, usually institutional money, and have specific rules on how they will invest those resources.

Similar to how there are different types of lenders and Angel investors, there are also different types of VCs and PE firms. Some are early investors that compete with Angel investors or may provide more funding than Angel investors. Generally, an early-stage venture capital firm is looking for the next new, great Big Idea. If your Big Idea is not large enough, in terms of scope and market reach, a VC may not be interested.

Some venture capitalists invest in ideas that have been proven and now need capital to expand the business. And some VCs fund more mature businesses that may be preparing for an initial public offering (IPO). PE firms focus on established companies and do not work with startups.

In addition, VCs and PE firms have specific areas of interest. It could be a single industry, a specific geographic location, or a particular type or size of company. These firms have specific guidelines to be met, so it is important that you understand what their requirements are.

> **The investment community is a very collegial group. They know, work, and socialize with one another, so asking for referrals can be helpful.**

Evan G. MacQueen, a venture capitalist with Core Capital Partners, states that if you are looking for funding, "Start with researching the investors you are interested in, as well as the deals they have done. Study their portfolio companies before meeting with them. Getting referred is the best approach and law firms that work on financing deals are a good resource."

The National Venture Capital Association states in its 2012 Yearbook: "Of every 100 companies who approach venture capitalists, 10 or less may get a serious look and only one company may be funded."[27]

It is important to note, if your company's concept projects only 10-20 percent growth or it is something that already exists, you may not get a close look from a venture capital firm. Be aware that the activity level within the U.S. venture-capital industry is only about half of what it was at its 2000-era peak. In 2011, there were 3,722 venture capital deals. Of these deals, one-third was handled by early-stage companies, another one-third were focused on expansion, and the final one-third were devoted to later-stage entities.[28] You need to truly evaluate your company's current situation and its projections for growth before approaching a venture-capital firm.

## How Your Proposal is Reviewed

Venture capitalists expect a short and simple presentation. Evan MacQueen[29] stated that at your first meeting, the PowerPoint presentation should be 10 slides. The main points you make include:

- A well-defined "who you are" and "what you do."

- State the idea briefly and concisely.

- Show how big the market is and the clients you have.

- Your business model, from the unit level to how growth stacks up in your forecast.

- Historical and projection graphs of revenues.

- What round, how much, and what reason.

He adds that afterwards, if they show interest, you can follow-up with the detail.

Funding sources are most likely to read your written proposal in the following order:

- Executive Summary

  - They look to see if you have a viable business plan and whether there is a big enough market for your products and services.

- Financials

  - They will determine whether you have realistic projections and whether you meet the requirements set by that particular funding source.

- Management

  - Financing sources are interested in the experience and abilities of the team responsible with carrying out the plan. Has it done this before and been successful? If not, does it have the experience and skill sets that may allow it to be successful in the future? Many funding sources say that the management team is even more important than the big idea.

- Exit Opportunity

  - Funding sources want to know whether your plan clearly outlines how the investor will make a sizeable profit on its investment.

Funding sources seek answers to each of the above topics. The next chapters help you learn how to adequately address them in your proposal.

## What Makes Funding Sources Less Interested to Invest

Lenders and investors have a number of issues that come through as their most frequent complaints. These include:

- Inadequately prepared proposals/business plans.

- Management teams lacking skills and experience.

- Unclear expansion strategy.

- Poor recordkeeping and reporting.

- Business owners with no "skin in the game" (a term financing sources use often and it means your personal investment).

- Business owners who take too much money out of the business.

- Businesses known for poor customer service (potential for business losses).

- Businesses in the wrong location.

- No or poor guidelines and requirements for customer credit processes.

- Poor management of inventory.

- Applications for businesses with whom the funding source does not work.

For a superior presentation to an investor, review each of the above points thoroughly and be prepared to deal with each of these issues. Having complete answers for each of the hard questions is imperative and will put you ahead of your competition.

## Successful Entrepreneurs Create Scarcity

There are many twists and turns in the funding process, which can take an inordinate amount of time with no decision being made. This is the major frustration for entrepreneurs. A single meeting with an investor is but a point in time. You will meet a number of times, building the relationship, providing more detail regarding the deal, etc.

But how long is too long?

Mark McGovern notes that "There is no rush from investors to give money, unless they feel they will be blocked from a great deal."[30] In many cases, an investor will not commit unless you can show that you are closing with a funder for a specific amount of money. Then they get serious.

Steve Kaplan adds, "To finalize a deal, you need to create a sense of scarcity—a 'buy today' mentality. You need to catalyze your investors, but it is a lot like herding cats."[31]

Also entrepreneurs hear contradictory strategies: keep knocking on doors; it is the guy who keeps knocking who gets the money. Or they hear all the VCs know each other, so if you talk to everybody, that is too much, and everybody will pass on it.

What is the right strategy? It is based on thorough research: which firms are right for you and your business model. Noel Glass says that "You want to be a red-hot deal and have two to three firms fighting for your business. That means you have to solve real problems. Get away from ethereal concepts and articulate the value you provide and show that people are willing to pay for it."[32]

## What Both Sides Say

When considering equity funding, look at it like a marriage with no divorce option. Both the entrepreneur and the investor are in it for the long haul. When speaking to both sides, it appears that neither side is totally happy with the final deal terms. Each side feels that they "could have done better." So keep that in mind as you are going through this process.

## Summary

Financing sources want the same thing you want, and that is to work with well-run businesses and make money. The way you manage your business will determine the success of your company, your bottom line, and whether you will obtain adequate funding to help you grow.

Your research will show you that lenders and investors have areas of specialty, and they each look for different kinds of information when they are evaluating your request. Or they may put different levels of priority on specific types of information. Your job is to identify each financing source's criteria before you present a proposal or make a presentation.

Building relationships with funding sources is a key part of building a business's growth plan. Start developing those relationships today. Ask your advisors, friends and colleagues to help get you introduced to both lenders and investors. Then learn what the funding sources want, and whether they are the right financing sources for you and the future of your business.

# The 10 Secrets to Winning Business Financing

# Chapter 8

# Secret #1

# Show You Are the 'A' Team

*"Great things in business are never done by one person. They're done by a team of people."*

~ Steve Jobs

Financing sources want to fund exceptional management teams. Experience shows that superior teams will get resources over groups that just have a great idea and well-written business plan.

A management team with a solid history of success makes financing sources feel more comfortable about their ability to execute. No matter how great your forecasts and business plan strategies, what makes a true winner is effective execution—and that's what a first-class management team provides.

A winning track record lessens the risk factors for both lenders and investors. A team with the right skills, experience, and capabilities to effectively implement stated goals and objectives is what funding sources expect.

Your goal is to communicate effectively to your potential funding source your team's high level of experience, skills, relationships, motivation and commitment. Show the funding source that you are a low risk because you have the ability and drive to successfully implement your business plan.

## What Makes You Different

Your goal in business is to show how your products and services are unique and satisfy a customer's needs. In dealing with financing sources, you also need to differentiate yourself. You want to show them why they need to "buy" you.

A history of solid achievement and success is a major differentiator. In addition, a highly skilled management team can mean the difference between success and failure in obtaining financing to grow your business.

Whether you have an "A" team or are in the process of building one, you have to do more than just highlight them in your presentation to a financing source. You need to spell out in detail what each member achieved and how that will help with the growth of your company. This is the place where you want to wow funding sources with the magic you bring to the table that will make them money.

In many presentations, I see uninspiring resumes of the management team. Instead of stating, for example, that you have 20 years as a marketing executive with ABC Corporation, provide the reader with a detailed, stimulating description of each member's successes. Specify their experience in terms of revenue growth, cost savings, increased profitability, and/or successful product launches for which each executive was responsible.

In your funding proposal, include detailed resumes that highlight the skills that key staff have which have helped your company's growth and profitability. It is important to detail specific, successful business experiences throughout their careers and translate that to how it is helping your company grow. Financing sources will have much more confidence in your business if the team has the experience to not only run the business effectively, but also to exceed stated goals that you have presented.

Excite the funding source about the caliber of your team. To do that, highlight your successes in inspiring language. For example:

- Turned around an underperforming company by redesigning the business model and strategy. Grew revenue by 20 percent and profitability by 100 percent in 18 months.

- Established innovative software company which grew to 200 clients and $1.5 million in sales within two years and was sold for $10 million.

- Delivered 180 percent sales increase after transforming company's approach to retail promotions. Created 20 account-specific, co-marketing programs for major retailers.

- Replaced $1 million in lost revenue due to downturn by revamping company's eCommerce site. Within one year, increased online sales by 100 percent and cut marketing costs by 46 percent with new online strategies.

## Building an "A" Team

Financing sources want to see an "A" team—members that have extensive experience and a solid track record of success in helping companies grow. Lenders and investors look to the skills and experience of the management team as the essential key to the success of the business. Lenders and investors pay significant attention to the management section of your proposal.

Funding sources commonly say they make their decisions more on the team than the business plan. In every conversation, lenders and investors noted the significance of the team, stating comments such as:

- "We buy the people, not the project."

- "If they are too difficult to deal with, we won't consider them."

- "If the team hasn't worked together long or seems not to like each other, big doubts are raised."

- "If they are arrogant, with very large egos, we won't deal with them."

To feel comfortable, funding sources want to see talent throughout the business. They want to be sure that you, as the firm's leader, can focus on the critical issues of the company and that you can rely on a strong team to manage the more day-to-day matters of the organization. They may believe that without a team backing you up, you would be squandering your time and as a result you would be less productive and, therefore, the company would be less profitable.

Identify strategies that show your company has the right people, with the right skills and capabilities at every level within the business. This can be accomplished even if you are a sole practitioner or micro-business. Should you be seeking financing for additional hires, detailing specifically how these positions are essential to growing the business must be part of your conversations with financing sources, as well as in your proposal.

When presenting the skills of your team, concentrate on each team member's skills and areas of expertise which offer the greatest contribution to the operation of the business. For all the key managers in the company, specifically outline the role that they play in growing the business.

## Show Talent at All Levels

Show the depth and breadth of the levels within your organization. If your company is very lean, one way to address this issue is to add the firm's advisors to the management team listing. For example, if you have an IT consultant setting up your systems, you might want to list her/him as part of your team. The same can be done with other consultants or advisors that you use to build your company.

If you have part-time staff or consultants, or someone who advises on a *pro bono* agreement, add them to your management skills listing. Make your CPA, legal counsel, and financial consultant, or other professional who works with your business, advisors to your management team. Always ask permission before adding them to your presentation. Be sure to identify the specific individuals as full-time employees, consultants, or advisors so that financing sources do not feel misled on the composition of the team they are backing.

Build the perception that your business has a strong team in place. This is important in the community at large, among your clients and prospects, as well as with potential financing sources. This will help grow your business and win financing.

Having the "A" management team does not always ensure that people view you as such; therefore, self-promotion is essential. Convincing communications should be part of your program. Writing articles for professional and/or trade organizations can help create word-of-mouth buzz for you and your company. These articles are a healthy supplement to your proposal.

It is very important to build the perception that you and your team are experts. Whether you establish yourself as the authority on search engine optimization at Google or the expert of the floral market in the local area, you will benefit by having the perception of being the expert in your field. Getting speaking engagements that position you as the expert is very helpful in building the perception that your team is golden. Providing a list of speaking engagements by members of the firm is also a good addition to your proposal and highlights the caliber of the management team.

> **A superior management team will get more resources and consideration over a group that just has a great idea and a well-written business plan.**

## Getting More Expertise

To be successful in business, take advantage of experts to augment your areas of expertise. Many entrepreneurs and small business owners have fallen into the trap of thinking they have to be an expert in all categories. In fact, that may be the reason for many small business failures. As stated previously, five of every 10 companies fail in the first five years. Only one-third of businesses make it to the 10-year point. So take advantage of those experts to expand your specific areas of expertise and increase your chances of success!

Identify experts in a variety of areas. Hiring experts is important, especially for small businesses that cannot afford to bring on full-time personnel. This can be done in myriad ways, from hiring consultants to building an advisory team. But this means you need to take an objective review of the skills of each member of your team and identify those skills that are missing. This could range from finance to logistics to IT—whatever it is that you need to have, experts can be consultants, contract personnel or part of your advisory team.

## Advisory Committee

No matter the size of your company, you can benefit by having an advisory committee. Its composition can include professionals from a variety of industries and backgrounds to help you in the planning and execution of your business plan. This also shows financing sources that you have a very mature view of your business.

It can be difficult to secure financing for a sole practitioner or a micro-business. Lenders and investors believe that investing in a company that small is a highly risky proposition. Financing sources will expect you to present how the company will pay the debt in case something happens to the one or two people who run it. This may be too high of a risk hurdle for some lenders and investors; however, an advisory team can be very advantageous in this situation.

An advisory committee can be a powerful asset in growing your business and can make a huge difference when you need to get objective advice. They are great to help you scout out the marketplace or to gauge future trends. An advisory committee can also help you with your strategic planning and, more importantly, with making introductions to potential clients, suppliers, and consultants. It can also be a referral into a financing source to help you get the money that you need to grow your business.

An advisory committee is not a board of directors or a corporate board. An advisory committee does not have fiduciary responsibility and its advice is nonbinding. Most entrepreneurs use these committees to play an advisory, evaluative, or devil's advocate role, which is important when you don't have a large management team. An advisory committee can include all types of business professionals, investors, interested outsiders, even customers or other successful business owners.

> **If your company's team is very lean, one way to address this issue is to form an advisory committee.**

To have an effective advisory committee, set the objectives of what you want to achieve. Is it going to be a general advisory group? Or do you need help in targeted areas, such as marketing, opening new markets, adopting new technology or improving operations? Or do you need an advisory committee to help you with a targeted issue? (For example, getting objective input on a business plan or getting the money you need to expand your business).

Selecting the right people to be part of your advisory committee is essential. That means understanding what skills you are seeking, skills that will augment your particular areas of expertise. Look for problem-solvers who have specific knowledge of business functions or deep industry expertise (e.g., new media). Some firms look for well-known people to give them credibility. This may be important if you are going after investment money. Overall, you want people who will spend the time getting to know your business, are well-connected, and are willing to make introductions. Your specific goals will determine the kind of person that you need to tap to be a member of your advisory committee.

Once you determine who should be on your advisory committee, the next step is to set its specific parameters. Outline what is expected, in terms of time commitments, responsibilities, as well as length of term on the committee. Consider having them sign confidentiality agreements if you will be sharing privileged information with them. This includes patents, intellectual property, proprietary processes, and systems.

If you do require individuals to sign documents to be part of the advisory group, you should also provide some amount of compensation to them as this may be necessary to make the legal contract binding in your state. While advisory committee members are not in this for the money, at a minimum, you should cover their cost for attending the meetings and provide for meals.

If you compensate each member, doing so as a per-meeting fee is best. This fee may range from a few hundred to a few thousand dollars, depending on the size and profitability of your company. Some companies also provide stock to their members. Before you do so, talk to your accountant and attorney to discuss the tax and legal implications.

Before establishing an advisory committee, make sure you have time to adequately prepare for meetings. This means developing agendas, providing important information before the meetings and managing the meetings. It is not effective for everyone to just show up without being prepared. Distribute minutes listing decisions and recommendations made to keep everyone at the same knowledge level.

Encouraging openness and honesty in meetings is essential for a good working relationship. Your advisory committee is actually giving you the benefit of their skills, experience and knowledge level, and, in some cases, contacts and referrals; in turn, they should be respected. Encourage your advisory committee to be your company's evangelist.

Respect the time of each and every advisory committee member. Do not feel that you always must have on-site meetings. Use technology such as conference calls, emails and Skype to keep them excited, updated, and informed. Listen to what each member has to say.

You do not have to implement everything the committee suggests, however. This is your business and you have the final say, but if you do not listen, they will not play as important a role as they could.

Business owners that have effective advisory committees have credited them with helping to deal with the hard issues, such as cutting costs, helping with product development, and introducing them to valuable clients, investors, and suppliers. The most important role they play is eliminating that sense of isolation that can come with running your own business. In that same vein, a very crucial role that an advisory committee can provide for a chief executive is to make you answerable to an objective third-party.

## Establishing a Board of Directors

Depending on the structure of your business, you may be required to establish a board of directors. If your business is structured as an S Corporation or C Corporation, you are required by law to have a board of directors. Also, if you are expecting to receive equity funding, you must form a board on which your investors will have a seat. An advisory committee differs from a board of directors because a board has legal decision-making authority for an organization and members may have legal liability in the event of investor losses.

Be sure to consult with an attorney when forming a board of directors so that you conform to your state's requirements, the requirements based on your articles of incorporation, and your corporate bylaws. There are some basic requirements with which boards must comply. They must hold at least one annual meeting and include a president, secretary and treasurer, but that may vary based on your state's requirements and your bylaws. The board must maintain written records of items and actions discussed at the meeting or have a signed statement approving the outcome and its actions.

If you are funded by an Angel investor or a venture capital firm, they usually require you to form a board on which they will be an active participant. As president of the business, you will assume the role of chairman of the board and CEO. The board is responsible for the CEO's compensation and can fire and replace the CEO as necessary. Board meetings tend to occur more frequently since investors have a more direct hand in strategic decisions for the company.

### *Working with a Board of Directors*

A board of directors can help your business by adding to and complementing the skills and expertise that you might not have in-house. A well-selected board can also help ensure that you have the right processes in place to manage growth and focus your strategy. The board can be helpful when preparing to raise capital and is essential when you are planning for an IPO (Initial Public Offering).

When establishing a board of directors, consider a broad range of people, including attorneys, CPAs, executives from other businesses, educators, and even directors from other boards. Look for people with expertise in the kind of business you operate. That usually makes it easier to bring board members up to speed. But it is also important to have people who represent other industries to give you an idea of what's happening outside your particular business parameters.

When you are establishing your board of directors, seek people who do not think exactly like you in all circumstances and are not afraid of standing up to you with their ideas. Look for influential people who have a good deal of experience either in your industry, in a particular function (for example, many firms look for IT executives), or just business in general.

Create a recruitment plan for your board. First, ask yourself what roles your business currently lacks, and what would be most valuable to move your company forward. This might be in the area of marketing, technology, or distribution or whatever your business is missing.

Outline how the board will function and what they will be responsible for. Is their role to audit the company, obtain investors, or raise outside capital? The function of the board needs to be specifically spelled out. Next, identify how often your board will meet. The average company meets with its board on a quarterly basis, but every company's needs are different. Identify what you need in your particular situation.

Outline how long they will serve. Typical terms are anywhere from one to three years. Many companies have set term and age limits. You can talk to your attorney about what is usual and customary in your particular area. Your industry trade and professional organizations can also provide detailed information for you to follow.

> **A board of directors can help your business by adding and complementing the skills and expertise you might not have in-house.**

Be prepared to explain the responsibilities of the board position and the time commitment involved. This is usually the first question asked when you approach someone to consider a position on your board. Each person will want to know what is expected and it is your role to detail the requirements upfront.

Boards are usually compensated. Compensation varies based on company size, meeting frequency, and other variables. At the very least, you should consider paying your directors on a per-meeting fee basis, which could run several hundred dollars or it could be set as an annual retainer. Talk to your CPA and your attorney to determine what would be best for your organization.

### *Recruiting Board Members*

Start the recruitment process by speaking with your attorney, CPA, or consultant. They may have suggestions. Network with businesses that have boards in place and ask them how they found their members. Also, don't forget Chambers of Commerce and your Small Business Development Centers (SBDC), which may provide you with good potential candidates.

If you do not know these people personally or professionally, checking references is important. Your trade or professional groups may have information for you on what is usual and customary in your industry, or talk to other executives in companies that have boards and ask them how they handle board recruitment.

## Summary

There is probably no better education for a business owner than working with a board of directors or an advisory committee to learn how to solve the challenges that a company has to deal with and learn about other industries. This enhanced knowledge can expand your skills, capabilities and reach into the industry and help your organization grow.

Additionally, boards can open up whole new personal networks for you and your company that will include CEOs, CFOs, consulting partners and other business leaders. This is an invaluable resource that you can tap for your business. Also, members of the board have another dividend and that is recruiting talent. For example, if one of your board members is a well-regarded college or business school professor, he/she may have their top students and top former students reach out to discuss job opportunities.

Some businesses, however, are not prepared for the time and energy commitments necessary in preparing for meetings and managing a board of directors or an advisory committee. Weigh the benefits and disadvantages of establishing a board or advisory committee based on your current situation.

# Chapter 9

# Secret #2

# Purpose of Your Request: Communicate How Your Success Will Make Them Money

*"Coming together is a beginning;*
*Keeping together is progress;*
*Working together is success."*

~ Henry Ford

P*ut your ASK in gear* was the mantra at a training session I attended many years ago. It is a great trigger reminding us what we must do to grow our businesses. We always have to ask—for the business, the referral, the testimonial, as well as for the financing.

But the differentiator here is the "how." How you ask a financing source for a loan or their investment can make the difference between a yes or no to your request for funding.

In an interview with *INC magazine*, Bob Seiwert, a senior vice president of the American Bankers Association who has thirty years of small-business banking experience, said it best when he stated, "One thing to realize as you're sitting down with a financial expert is that, well, you aren't one. Most entrepreneurs are enthusiastic risk-takers." He continued to say that the way to impress a financing source is to come prepared. "Arm yourself with financial statements as well as proforma projections so the bank can get an idea of where your business is going." Seiwert suggests including not only the rosiest scenario, but the most-likely case, and a worst-case projection. He says, "The banker will see, ah, this business owner really has their ducks in order."[33]

Showing your potential financing source that you really understand your business and the potential upsides and downsides that your business may face in the future is important. Moreover, demonstrating that you are open to disclosing such opportunities and risks with your potential financing partner is critical.

## The Funding Request

The funding request is a statement of how much money you need, why you need it, how you are going to invest the proceeds, and what the future returns will be to the financing source. There are some differences between a lender request and an investor request.

In the case of a lender request, detail how the lender will be repaid for the amount borrowed plus interest. Investors want to know the potential return on their equity investments. They want to understand how they will be rewarded in the future for having taken a risk on investing in your business today. In order for equity investors to be rewarded, they have to sell their equity investment. Nearly all Angel investors, VCs, and PE firms are not buy-and-hold investors. They want liquidity on their stock holding, which means an exit strategy must be developed before they invest in your business.

An exit strategy could include an IPO, merger, sale of the company, or stock redemption. Or you could plan for the company to buy back its stock after it has grown.

Your investors, however, will be looking to maximize the value of their shares, and that could mean a significant increase in the value that you will pay to them compared to the initial investment. Work with your financial and legal advisor to determine what the typical wealth creation/liquidity event is most likely for your company and how business values are typically determined within your industry.

When approaching a lender or investor with a request for money, you must provide a written proposal and an oral presentation. Remember, they are interviewing you and you are interviewing them to be long-term partners. This is not something to go into lightly.

## Show That You Have Prepared Well

"You have to be prepared," said Robert Seiwert, in an interview in the *Dayton Business Journal*. "If you have a viable business model and the banker feels that this business model is going to work in this new economy, you have a very good chance of getting financing. But you have to be ready to show that it will work."[34]

Lenders and investors want to know you have planned appropriately. Before approaching a funding source, determine how much you actually need—working capital, as well as capital for investments. The next step is to identify and prioritize the capital investments that increase the business's value.

Clearly and briefly state what you want in the cover letter and the executive summary: for example, if you are approaching a lender, specifically state (examples in parentheses):

- Amount Requested ($100,000)

- Type of Financing (loan, line of credit, loan for equipment)

- Interest Rate (Prime plus 2 percent)

- Length of Financing (5 years)

- Method of Repayment (monthly repayment amortized over 5 years paid from the firm's profit)

- Collateral (company's owners offer a second mortgage on a residence with an estimated equity of $150,000)

To help you develop your financing request, there is a very good template which has been created by the Service Corps of Retired Executives (SCORE). They have produced a template for an Executive Summary and placed it on the Microsoft tem-plate site. (Download at http://office.microsoft.com/enus/templates/bank-loan-request-letter-TC001017547.aspx.) You can review this template created by SCORE at the end of this chapter.

Always keep in mind that this presentation is a major marketing endeavor; however, many times, the actual request is treated as an after-thought. It is listed as XX number of dollars for a loan, line of credit, equipment lease or purchase. To be a winner in this race, you need to do much more. The purpose must be a dynamic statement which sets the tone for the entire presentation.

"People do not buy for logical reasons. They buy for emotional reasons," says Zig Ziglar, a well-known sales expert.[35] And financing sources are no exception. Always remember, the loan officer and funding committee members are human beings. They must be excited and motivated to help you succeed and your company to grow.

There are some differences in how you approach a lender versus an investor. The lender wants to know how you will repay the loan in a timely fashion. The investor is looking for a significant return on their investment and will be looking to see your exit strategy. This information must be presented in the cover letter and executive summary.

## Financing Request to a Lender

When approaching a lender you will need to provide an Executive Summary. Some lenders may require a separate "Term Sheet," which specifically states the amount requested, the preferred type of financing, the interest rates and length of term, as well as the method of repayment. Usually, this information is presented as part of the Executive Summary.

Always give the lender what they want in the format that they require. Be sure to ask what they prefer and follow their instructions precisely.

### *The Cover Letter to a Proposal for a Lender*

You should always include a cover letter on company letterhead to any proposal. Include the:

- Date you are delivering the proposal to the lender.

- Your business contact information.

  - Name of primary contact and position

  - All contact information: phone, email address, physical address

- Amount of the financing requested.

- Uses of the money requested.

  - Real estate, equipment purchase, working capital, additional hires

- Type of loan.

    – Debt, fixed term installment, line of credit

- Proposed interest rate listed as fixed or variable.

    – Prime plus X percent, maximum XX percent, or a fixed rate for a certain term

- Requested term (months or years).

    – Fixed for 5 years

- Closing date (when you want the money).

    – June 1, 20XX

- Repayment schedule beginning and end.

    – Begins 30 days after receipt of funds
    – Ends May 30, 20XX (5 years)

- Collateral

    – Receivables, inventory, real estate, stock

- Guarantees

    – Business and, if necessary, personal

- Sources of repayment funds

    – Cash flow after operations

- Fees

    – As needed

Similar to working with a potential client in your business, this proposal is to start the conversation. The bank will come back to you with changes. For example, after you request a fixed 5 percent loan for 5 years, the response may come back that the bank is interested to provide your business with a variable rate loan at a higher interest rate for a shorter period of time. From there, the negotiations can continue, but each side understands "the ask" requirements of the other side.

### The Executive Summary for a Lender

This section is a brief digest—one to three pages—which provides the lender with all the required information. This section will include the:

- Name of the business.

- Brief description of the business, including the products and services offered.

- Mission statement for the business.

- Date the business began.

- Name of management team and functions within the business.

- Number of employees.

- Brief description of the business facilities and physical assets.

- Amount you wish to borrow.

- How the money will be used.

- Type of financing requested.

- Payment schedule and source of repayment.

- Collateral offered:

  - Financial performance summaries

  - Historical financials for 1-5 years (if available)

  - Projected financials for 3-5 years (minimally, the term of the loan)

A sample executive summary is presented at the end of this chapter.

### Show How the Money Will Be Used

Provide a description of how you will invest the proceeds of the loan and provide commentary on how this will be beneficial to the company's growth and profitability. For example, state the benefits in terms that a financial expert will understand:

> *ABC Company will use the $500,000 of proceeds from the loan to buy a widget maker. With this piece of equipment, ABC Company can increase its volume of widgets to meet customer demand which has grown by 20% over the last three quarters, and is forecasted to increase at the same pace for the next three years. In addition, this equipment will bring costs down by 14%. ABC Company will repay the loan in three years from the cash flow from operations based on the increased revenue and increased profitability from the acquisition and operation of the widget maker.*

A differentiating feature of a winning proposal is that the request details how the loan enhances the business. Always state how these funds will help the company's:

- Growth

- Productivity

- Profitability

- Cash Flow

### Requests for Working Capital

Lenders can be wary of requests for working capital, and this may actually raise a red flag. The lender may question if the business can repay debt if it does not have enough cash to operate the business.

An experienced lender will want to know if your business has problems collecting receivables, has over-produced inventory, cannot sell inventory, or bought too much or overpriced equipment. Be prepared to provide information about your business and the reason for the loan before the lender has to ask. Financing sources will appreciate the information you provide upfront, not only to show your honesty, but also to show your strong knowledge of the business.

Many lenders have working capital minimums that must be achieved before they will lend money to a business for certain loans. Also, lenders may require that current assets exceed current liabilities and may look for a current ratio greater than a 1 to 1. The higher the ratio, the more liquid the company; lenders like lots of liquidity. Financial ratios are detailed in Chapter 12. That said, there are always exceptions to the rule. Identifying exceptions requires communicating with potential funding sources about their requirements and about the operations of your business.

The purpose of the request is to clearly explain how this money will improve your company's operations, increase revenue, profitability, and cash flow within a specific timeline. All this leads to the biggest question from the lender: how will they be repaid.

## Funding Request to an Investor

Before contacting an equity investor, identify which type you should pursue: Angel investors, venture capital firms that invest in ideas or early-stage businesses, or private equity firms or buyout groups that invest in established companies.

Are you seeking equity capital for an established, operating business? If so, identify private equity firms or groups that do buy-outs. Or, are you seeking equity capital for a Big Idea that needs funding to pursue the realization of your idea? If so, identify Angel Investors and venture capitalists.

If you have an established, operating business, some initial questions to consider are the following:

- Are you seeking an equity investor to invest capital directly in your business for growth?

- Do you want to sell a portion of your company to diversify your personal portfolio because nearly all of your personal wealth is tied up in the illiquid stock of your company?

- If so, do you want to sell a minority position in your company or are you interested in a new partner who wants to own a majority stake in your business?

If you are not an established, operating company, but you do have a Big Idea that needs equity capital to pursue the growth of your idea:

- How much capital do you need to prove your idea works or complete a prototype?

- How much ownership are you willing to sell?

Equity investors (private equity firms, Angels, and VCs) have significant opportunity to invest in a large number of businesses, but they generally invest in one percent or less of the opportunities they evaluate. Differentiate yourself from the multitude of businesses that are asking for their support. First and foremost, determine which investors focus on businesses such as yours. If your business meets the investment criteria set by investors, they may be interested to learn about your business. As discussed earlier, it is best to have made personal contact with investors about your business before sending your written proposal.

Your proposal should describe your business (or the Big Idea that you intend to pursue); the significant market opportunity that you are going after (including quantitative detail about the market size and your potential market share); your management team (with experience and skills to execute the plan); as well as historical and projected financials.

In addition, investors like to know that you have skin in the game, so emphasize what you are personally investing in the business. Assure investors that their investment is well worth the risk and you are committed to the success of the business.

### Cover Letter for an Investor

Include a cover letter on letterhead, which lists:

- Date delivered to the investor.

- Your business contact information.

    - Name of primary contact

    - Position

    - Phone number(s)

- email address

- physical address (include mailing address, if different

- Business description (or detail of your Big Idea and the business model you will pursue).

- Amount of the funding request.

- Uses of the money requested.

- Benefits to the Investor.

### *Executive Summary for an Investor*

It is imperative that the executive summary captures the investors' attention and motivates them to reach out to you because they want to learn more. This section should be brief and summarize your Big Idea, the business model, and how the management team will successfully execute the plan.

Clearly state how much funding you need. Describe how the funds will be used and highlight how the funds will generate revenues. Investors are interested in helping to build new companies, as well as creating wealth. Detail how your venture will both create an exciting, high growth company and provide a large return on their investment.

The executive summary should include the:

- Name of the business and contact information.

- Brief description of the business, including the products and services offered.

- Mission statement.

- Company history.

- Management team experience and relevant skills.

- Number of employees.

- Amount of request.

- Use of funds.

- Business model.

- Current investors and lenders.

- Historical and projected financials.

For start-up businesses, you may not have much of this information available because you do not have a business history. In that case, focus more on the experience and track record of the management team. Also, provide highlights of the research on which you based your forecasts, and reasons for starting the business. Clearly define the need you have discovered and how your solution solves the problem.

## Summary

Your financing request is one of the most important pieces of your proposal. If you do not excite the lender or investor at the beginning, your request will end up in the round file (also known as the trash can). You will be judged by your writing and your presentation package. You may want to get some professional help to make your proposal top notch.

# Sample Executive Summary

To help you develop your financing request, here is a sample of an executive summary created by the Service Corps of Retired Executives (SCORE). As stated previously, it can be downloaded at:

http://office.microsoft.com/en-us/templates/bank-loan-request-letter-TC001017547.aspx

## Executive Summary

ADVENTURE WORKS is a high-end design and remodeling firm with a reputation for integrity, quality craftsmanship, and excellence in management. In three years annual sales have increased to be well over a million dollars.

ADVENTURE WORKS was formed by Brian Groth as a Sole Proprietorship in December 1997. In 1998 a combination of activities involving residential design, consulting, and general construction brought Gross Sales of $250,000.

The Company experienced steady growth since its inception, and incorporated in March 1999, (see Appendix 6, Articles of Incorporation). In 1999 Gross Sales of $750,000 were achieved. In 2000, signed contracts show that Gross Sales are expected to be $1,300,000 (see Appendix 2, current Backlog).

The Company has its address in leased premises at 1234 A Street, Springfield, MD 40523. Its activities fall under the Standard Industrial Classification SIC 1521 and 1522. The owners are Brian Groth and Julie Bankert.

ADVENTURE WORKS is involved in four distinct activities:

1. Architectural Design
2. Residential & Light Commercial Construction
3. Property Services
4. Retail Floor Coverings (see Appendix 4).

Eighty to ninety percent of the Gross Sales are in design and construction. At the moment (May 2000), there are 25 permanent employees on the payroll and 10 subcontracted workers excluding subcontracting companies (see Appendix 1 for resumes).

The company's Short Term Objectives (within the next three years) are to increase activity in all Divisions, and to achieve annual profit, net after taxes, of $200,000 by 2005. Its Long term objectives are: to maintain the level of current business achieved up to 2005, and then to move into historical restorations, more light commercial work, and increased new custom home construction.

To implement these objectives the company needs:

1.  A loan of $100,000 at Prime plus 2%. This loan to be used for current near term expenses including _____, _____ and _____. It will be repaid in five years.

2.  A line of credit of $50,000 to take advantage of discounts available, avoid associated penalties, and expand into high profit areas requiring positive cash flow.

The prospects for ADVENTURE WORKS' continued growth are excellent, with 2000 construction and design contracts underway already exceeding $550,000 (see Appendix 2, Backlog 2000).

For equity the company has assets of $227,000 (see Appendix 9, Balance Sheet as of mm/dd/2003). Additionally, the company's owners are willing to offer as collateral a second mortgage on a residence with an estimated equity of $150,000. The address of this residence is 456 Oak Dr., Mt. Vernon, CA 31304.

The company's overall objective is to satisfy that market segment that demands integrity and quality construction, and to maintain a steady growth in sales volume that will sustain the company for twenty years. Brian Groth has enhanced his reputation to the point where the company is regarded by many architects as the recommended choice with their clients due to the excellence of its craftsmen and management.

Market research shows that the population in Springfield has increased by 200,000 between 1985 and 2003. This increase in population brought about an increase of 19,850 new single family homes valued at over three billion dollars. This increase gives the area over 128,000 existing homes as a potential remodeling market. Demographic estimates published by the State Office of Financial Management, 2002, indicate that an additional 20,000 persons will need to be housed between 2002 and 2020. ADVENTURE WORKS intends to pursue this market vigorously. (See Appendix 7 for data on anticipated changes in the population of the County).

## Financial Objectives

The financial objectives of ADVENTURE WORKS over the next few years are as follows:

|  | **2005** | **2005-2010** |
|---|---|---|
| **Sales** | $7,000,000 | $10,000,000 |
| **Net Income after Tax** | $ 500,000 | $ 1,000,000 |

Please review the enclosed business plan and loan proposal, and of course feel free to ask for any additional information or explanations you may want. I will call you in about one week's time to arrange an appointment so that we can discuss the loan in person.

I look forward to a mutually profitable relationship with the Woodgrove Bank.

Sincerely,


Brian Groth

# Chapter 10

# Secret # 3

# Industry Trends and Your Business Opportunities

*"You cannot adjust the wind...*
*but you can adjust your sail."*

~ Axel Schultze

"**A** company lives and dies by its customers and clients," claims Dharmesh Shah, founder and CTO of HubSpot, a provider of inbound marketing software.[36] For your business to be successful, you must look to the future and think deeply about the opportunities presented by evolving trends. This must be part of your business plan, execution strategies, and presentation to funding sources.

When Wayne Gretzky was asked how he became the National Hockey League leading scorer, he said the trick was "skating to where the puck's going to be, not where it is." By anticipating the players' moves, he dynamically positioned himself to take the shot. This is exactly what your business needs to do—dynamically position itself to anticipate the market's direction and competitors' responses. That is one way strategic planning gives you an edge by focusing on where you need to be in the next year, three years, and up to five years in the future. This chapter discusses the research that needs to be done and how to complete that research in order to maximize your potential for success.

## Identify your Best Opportunities

Remember that financing sources review scores of business plans and financial requests each day. They are very educated as to the trends in the industries they work with.

Don't be surprised if they ask you questions regarding trends, threats, and opportunities. They will be testing you to see if you are on top of what is happening in your market and taking innovative steps to profit from the options available.

Your proposal should state your best opportunities in:

- Growing of current segments.
- Creating of new market segments.
- Cross-selling, up-selling, and bundling of products/services.
- Creating new products and services.
- Increasing capacity.

Base opportunities on accurate research. Funding sources want forecasts based on reasonable assumptions, including actual historical performance and future growth potential with your products and services, given the trends in the market.

Research is not just busy work that provides volume to your presentation. This research should help you identify options to increase your revenue and profitability. It will help you be successful in winning business financing and in becoming a more successful company than you currently are!

## Today's Drivers

Be aware that many factors can make or break your business. One factor is economic, such as the financial meltdown that impacted many companies worldwide. Regulatory issues can also create high hurdles to overcome. The biggest trends that affect us on a day-to-day basis fall into the demographic, geographic and technological arenas.

Demographic shifts impact business in myriad ways; for example, this is the first time in history that five generations are working side-by-side. Each of these segments operate in different ways, many times causing unneeded friction in the workplace. Can your business help in making it a smoother workplace?

So what is a demographic shift? It can be population growth; for example, if you live in an area with large immigration into your area and you are in real estate, this can be a boon to your business, if you implement the right strategies.

> *Many factors can make or break your business – economic, demographic, geographic, technological, or regulatory.*

The same can be said for geographic trends such as increasing urbanization and the ever-widening divide between youthful and quickly aging populations, not only here in America but also in many industrialized nations. We see the trend in other countries of a rapidly rising middle class. These trends are reshaping the world and can be a major driver for your business.

Today, even the smallest of businesses can be a player on the world stage. Due to the increasing need for products and services worldwide, and the expansion of the internet, your business should be looking at how to take advantage of these markets.

Today's biggest drivers seem to center around disruptive technological innovation. Whether you are the creator or the user of that technology, it is having massive effects on business and society as a whole. And the speed of those changes only seems to be increasing. Your focus needs to be on how you can take advantage of those changes to grow your business.

But these drivers also create huge challenges for each of us. Due to technological changes, we are dealing with more sophisticated consumers who are demanding much more of the businesses from whom they purchase. They can quickly provide positive or negative feedback in a very public forum online. The challenge is in developing new ways of clearly and positively communicating with this audience and persuading them to try our new products and services.

How can we take advantage of changing consumer demographics? In developing countries, there is a huge increase in populations over the age of 60. Research Now, states in its 2012 Global Reference Guide[37] that the U.S., Canada, and Australia have approximately 20 percent of their population over 60. Europe hovers in the mid-20 percent, while Japan's seniors number over 30 percent. In much of the developed world, the elderly represent an increasing portion of the population. On the other hand, young and middle-class populations are emerging in China, India and Russia, and much of South America. How can your business use this information as a growth platform?

The main goal of marketing is to serve consumers with constantly changing needs and requirements effectively while optimizing costs.

## Know Your Industry Trends

From working with hundreds of companies, I have found that the successful ones keep a focused eye on the trends affecting their customers. They also have a sharper eye on how the competition responds to those trends. Many small businesses cannot afford marketing research firms, but there are avenues to obtain that information in very cost-effective terms.

The first step is to talk to your customers and suppliers. They can provide you with the most current and effective information. Your trade and professional organizations can also provide reams of data. Executives of the large corporations often speak on topics relevant to your business' target markets. Even your local librarian can be a major source of information. You can Google for information online or hire an intern from the marketing program at a local university to do the research for you. There is no excuse for not keeping on top of trends. Remember, financing sources do keep on top of trends and will be making sure that you are as well.

## Conduct Research

As part of your business plan, you need to conduct research. This research will be essential in developing a business model that is best for your company. Effective research includes:

- Identifying your ideal customers.

- Locating your competition.

- Understanding trends affecting your specific industry and market.

- Determining your strengths and weaknesses.

133

There are some standard research strategies that your funding source may ask about. The first is a PEST review. **PEST** stands for **P**olitical, **E**conomic, **S**ocial, and **T**echnological review of trends that affect your business. This strategy helps you to identify and understand current and potential environmental factors that can affect your business and impact marketing strategies.

The most common research strategy is a **SWOT** analysis, which is a process you conduct to understand your company's internal **S**trengths and **W**eaknesses, as well as external **O**pportunities and **T**hreats in the marketplace. The goal of the SWOT analysis is to identify the critical factors affecting your business, build on your strengths to reduce your weaknesses, exploit opportunities, and avoid the potential threats. A major benefit of conducting the SWOT analysis is to use the results of the analysis as action programs that will help your company grow and succeed.

Your SWOT analysis can help you identify various factors influencing your business. For example, it may focus on:

- Strengths

  - Cost advantages over competitors
  - Best customer service in the industry
  - Strong customer retention
  - Recognition for social responsibility

- Weaknesses

  - Need for experienced managers to help growth
  - Inadequate financing for growth
  - Weak brand recognition in the market
  - High customer churn

- Opportunities
    - Growing demand for quality products in your market
    - Enter new geographic markets or client segments
    - Capture additional clients as your major competitor is losing clients
    - Acquire firms with needed technology
- Threats
    - Changing buyer tastes
    - Likely entry of new competitors
    - Cost of supplies increasing
    - Adverse government policies

Research is the planning, collecting, and analyzing of information related to making effective decisions and is essential in developing successful marketing strategies. It is vital to help you determine which market segments are optimal for your products and services and how to best position yourself to beat the competition.

Business and market research will assist you to:

- Identify prospective customers.
- Improve understanding current clients' needs.
- Discern the size and characteristics of specific markets.
- Set realistic goals and targets.
- Identify new opportunities.
- Formulate successful strategies.
- Develop solutions to business problems.

You can gather this information in two ways: primary and/or secondary research. Primary research is collecting data directly from your customers, suppliers, and other key stakeholders. Secondary data is information already available through reports, articles, and presentations, most of which you can easily find online.

Effective research will greatly help your business, but poor or inaccurate research can lead to bad marketing and business decisions. Approaching your research objectively to obtain truthful information, rather than just looking at data that reflects what you want it to be, is essential.

To conduct effective research, do the following:

- Identify Your Goal or Define the Issue

    - Research can be like a black hole eating up immense resources. Before you begin a research project, outline your objectives. Let's say you want to introduce a new product into the marketplace. The objectives could be taken step-by-step or in a comprehensive fashion by identifying:

        - The potential market size for this product or service (volume and price)

        - How clients would respond to this new offering

        - The potential costs for this new offering

        - The go-to-market plan

- Determine Your Research Strategy

    - By designing your research strategy upfront, you can save time and money. As stated, the two main sources of research include primary and secondary research.

- Primary research, while providing the best information, can be costly in time and dollars. It requires you to conduct interviews or surveys. If you do it yourself, it takes a lot of time, and if you outsource it to a research firm, it can be expensive. See if you can identify inexpensive ways to conduct the research. For example, you could set up a free survey on Survey Monkey (www.Survey Monkey.com) and send it to your current and/or potential customers.

- Secondary research can be more cost-effective and uses existing published information. Find this data online or approach universities, your industry or trade groups, research and government agencies, and experts.

- The best approach is to define the secondary information available then select specific areas in which to conduct primary research.

- Analyze the Data

  - Once you have compiled all the data, organize and evaluate it in relation to the objectives set. As you study the information, draw your conclusions and develop recommendations to formulate your marketing strategies.

  - As you evaluate the information collected, you may find that you need more data on particular aspects before making decisions, so you may have to conduct additional research.

- Prepare a Report

  – Best practices point to always preparing a written report on the outcomes of the research and the recommendations for action, even if you are doing it for yourself. First, put it into a structured report to ensure that the information is credible. Second, refer to it in the future and compare it with future research. Third, provide it to others to get them up to speed. Effectively communicating the research outcomes throughout the company is essential.

## Your Personal Storehouse of Information

The first place to start with any research project is the management team. If your managers are knowledgeable on your industry, you have a storehouse of information at your fingertips. The same can be said for your sales teams. On a regular basis, tap their knowledge and expertise by asking them to:

- Identify and prioritize key trends that are likely to affect the company.

- Outline strategies to take advantage of favorable trends.

- Develop approaches to minimize the impact of unfavorable trends.

The people in your company who are out in the field and those who have constant interactions with your customers, suppliers, and other key stakeholders have a great deal of information about trends affecting your company. They are your personal research staff—even though they may not know it. Take advantage of what they can bring to the table to make your organization very attuned to what is happening in the markets you service.

Together you can identify and respond to trends in the market by discussing the pattern of growth or decline in sales resulting from changes in environmental factors such as seasonality, population, social, technology, economic cycles and political climate.

## Summary

Funding sources are steeped in market trends and how to best use them to the advantage of business growth. They understand that trend analyses can provide information on growth and decline rates for overall markets and individual segments.

It is your responsibility to both identify and understand trends in your market to assist you in forecasting future sales and anticipating events and changes that can impact your business. You must be able to discuss short-, medium-, and long-term trends with your financing sources and show them how you can benefit from changes in the market.

Once you have identified your customers, competitors and the trends in the market, the next step would be to have a deep understanding how your products and services effectively benefit your marketplace. Identify past, present, and future trends of those products and services and the external factors and trends affecting them. Use this information to shape your strategy for growth.

# Chapter 11

# Secret # 4

# Eliminate Concentration and Increase Your Probability of Success

*"Customers are an investment. Maximize your return."*

~ PeopleSoft Ad

Y ou got the big client! You and your team cele-
brated the huge win and went about building the
business around servicing all the needs of that
customer. This client brought in huge revenues
and is the major reason for the growth of your business.
All is great—or is it?

Yes, it is great to continue to win clients and grow
your business with existing clients. Focusing on serving
your clients better than anyone else is the key to success. Having only one or two or even a few large clients
as the backbone of your business, however, may make it
more difficult for a financing source to gain comfort with
providing a loan to you or investing in your company.

The same can be said about significant concentration
with only one or two product or service offerings. If

something negative happens in the market or with your major offering, your business could be severely hurt in a short period of time.

It is important to review your company in terms of the benefits of minimizing concentration (client, vendor, and product) to maximize the value of your company, as well as to improve your ability to win business funding.

## The Risk

It can feel great to prosper with one or two major clients. They love your offerings and you enjoy working with them. You may even be personal friends. But the risk goes beyond financing sources. For your own protection, diversify by winning additional clients and minimizing the potential downside of client concentration.

If a single source of work provides 25 percent or more of your revenues, you may have a client concentration problem. If that client runs into financial trouble, you may lose a significant amount of your revenue if it reduces or stops its purchases. Your receivables are now at risk and you may not receive payment. Your future is now intertwined with the fate of your struggling client— a fate that you cannot control or manage.

Many possibilities can create negative situations. For example, an economic downturn may reduce your customers' purchasing ability. They could be losing their own customers, affecting their ability to purchase your products or services, or in a worse case, even be facing bankruptcy. The owner may retire or sell the business to a new entity. The new owners may want to change vendors. Be prepared for all situations.

This issue of concentration also applies to your major vendors. If, for example, you run a manufacturing firm and you source all of your raw materials from one vendor, your business is at risk. You may have leverage in negotiating a lower price if you purchase higher volume from one vendor; however, you have also tied the success of your business to the success of your vendor's business. If that vendor has a production or sourcing problem, you may not be able to secure the essential components needed for your products, which will impact your ability to generate revenue.

But this situation can happen to businesses in any sector. For example, a client in the health and wellness sector offers a specialty product. Her supplier is located in a northeastern state. When hurricane Sandy hit in 2012, her supplier's facilities were severely impacted by the rain, wind, and flooding. Her supply of the essential raw ingredient was cut off completely until the vendor could make the necessary repairs and began manufacturing again. The client was unable to generate any revenue based on a major product offering until finding another vendor. And, the client had limited negotiating leverage with the new vendor since there was now an emergency need to source the raw material. This is not a good situation for any business, and it demonstrates the risk of product concentration.

> *Overdependence on a single client, vendor, supplier, or offering is a major red flag to funding sources and may stop you from getting the financing you need.*

Similarly, you may have a successful business built on one product or service. That product or service may be doing well today, but there is a risk that if demand declines, your business may be negatively impacted. Such a drop in demand may have nothing to do with the quality you offer; rather, it may be due to a completely new product or service from a competitor or a change in regulations. Either may impact demand immediately or over time. If your revenue is generated through sales of multiple offerings, there is much less risk to your company if the demand for one product declines.

Though we covered the management team in more detail in Chapter 8, the same concentration risk applies if you don't have broad leadership team but depend completely on one or two people. If one of them were hit by the proverbial bus, would you be able to continue to run the business or would you have an issue with generating revenue or serving your clients? For this reason, your business benefits by having a bench of talented managers helping to grow the business.

Over-dependence on a single client, offering, or vendor is a major red flag to funding sources. If there is concern that one event could significantly impact the company in a negative way, lenders will be concerned about their ability to be repaid. Investors will question if they can make a profit on their investment. This is one reason why companies with concentration issues have difficulty obtaining financing. Minimizing concentration helps win business financing, as well as increases the value of a business.

While concentration can be an issue across a broad variety of areas, initially focusing on client concentration is important. Do a comprehensive analysis of your total customer base to ensure that you are diversified.

## Take a Look at Your Customer Base

Funding sources look at your entire customer base. Their goal is to determine your company's stability and potential for growth. Diversifying and expanding your client base is essential to increasing value in your firm.

Every business must focus on gaining new clients, as well as expanding the existing customer base by cross-selling and upselling its products and services. Examine your customer base and ask:

- What would be the impact on the business if our top customer(s) stopped buying?

- How "easy" would it be for a competitor to steal our top customer(s)?

- What keeps our top customer(s) here?

- Why would our top client go to a competitor?

- What can we do to lessen the concentration of our top clients?

- How can we increase business with our smaller clients or obtain new customers?

When considering these issues, focus on each question and determine how each point will impact the business.

How can you determine the impact of a key customer who stops buying? The easiest approach is to develop a Pro Forma budget for each customer that analyzes the historical and projected revenue, gross profit, and (if possible) profitability after corporate expenses, so you can truly understand your exposure should any of those clients leave you.

Many companies that conduct a deep analysis may find that certain large clients providing significant revenue do not contribute much profitability or may even contribute negative profitability. Determine if you can increase profitability with that client or even drop that customer to focus on higher-profitability clients.

"We all want our clients to love us," stated Sophia Brooks, CEO of Global Learning Partners, a national customer service training company, "however, customers won't if you give bad service—but your competitors surely will. Unless you provide practical solutions to mitigate a customer's pain, coupled with outstanding service and real value, you will always be vulnerable to having them lured away by the competition."

So review the solutions you provide to your customers versus those provided by the competition. Do you give them more than what they want? Do you make it easy for them to stay with you and harder for them to move to another company?

One of the best examples of providing practical solutions to clients is the commercial storage industry. For businesses, such as law firms, that have massive files that need to be kept for a proscribed period of time, commercial storage companies provide a solution to the aggravating problem of dealing with tons of paper. All the law firm wants is for you to pick up and deliver on time. The storage company can charge for each and every time they handle the law firm's goods. It is difficult for the law firm to change providers—moving tons of paper to another location is not an easy endeavor and not a decision one makes lightly. All the storage company has to do is a good job in responding to their clients' requests and they do not have to worry about their customers leaving. Think about your business today. Can you say the same about your products or services?

While your company's growth goals should always be on increasing and diversifying your client base, also focus on maintaining and expanding the client base you have. It generally takes 7 to 10 times more resources to bring in a new client than it does to maintain and expand a current client.[38] Also, it takes time to bring in new business in any industry. So take care of what you have, because it will take many more resources to replace it. And keeping clients really helps profitability.

If you could keep just five percent of the customers you normally lose, many sources state that you can increase your profitability significantly—25 to 95 percent![39]

In these uncertain financial times, anything can happen to a client. For example, how would your company fare if there was a change in ownership for your major customers? It is always a good habit to review any contracts you have in place to understand what would be involved if those companies did get new management.

- Can the contract stay in place with no change?

- Would you get written notice?

- Does it have language that will not allow assignment of your contract to the new owners?

You should understand the details of the relationship in the contracts you have, as well as any contracts you negotiate in the future.

## Lenders May Not Lend

One of my clients wanted to sell her business. She was able to attract a lot of interest; that is, until the potential buyers saw that 90 percent of her business was with just one client, a government agency. While an agency may have multiple decision-makers, which operate in multiple departments, in this case, the business was with one decision-maker. This client concentration scared away most potential buyers.

With fewer interested parties, the valuation was lower than the owner expected. The ultimate buyer refused to consider an all-cash deal and required a large portion of the purchase price to be paid over time based on the performance of the business (an earn-out). Since the earn-out payment was based on the future performance of the business, the owner continued to have some risk if the government agency reduced its purchase volume. This is a highly tenuous situation and happens more often than most business owners realize.

This can be a problem even if the work comes from a variety of departments within a company. It may even be from different managers within those departments, and the business owner feels secure. Despite this, your company can still be at risk as this is only one client and, as previously stated, that client can be affected by a variety of negative situations.

The fact is that customer concentration can be a very serious issue if you want to finance or sell your company. For example, one business owner that wanted to sell his business was working with three very interested parties. Each party spent time meeting with management and submitted bids to acquire the company. The lenders, however, refused to loan money to the buyers to finance the deal because of the lenders' concern with customer concentration.

Since the buyers could not get debt financing for the acquisition, the interested parties significantly reduced the value of their bids. The owner refused to sell at the lower value and had to delay the sale process until they could diversify their customer base.

If you are looking at SBA financing, be aware that on the loan application, there is a yes or no question: "Does any customer make up more than 10 percent of your accounts receivable?" If you check the "yes" box, the lender may raise questions. In some cases, checking that "yes" may lead to a "no" for a SBA-backed loan.

If you see this kind of customer concentration issue in your business, it is imperative to create and execute a plan on how to change it before you begin the process of seeking financing or selling your business.

The truth is that you can lose a client in ways that you cannot plan for or foresee. This can include the following:

- Merger or Acquisition

    - Once this occurs, the rule is that all relationships are reviewed, and many vendors are renegotiated or replaced.

- Change in Management

    - New managers may bring in their own teams and want to bring in a different vendor.

- Consolidation of Suppliers

    - The trend today is away from managing a large number of suppliers. Many large companies are consolidating on all fronts. Some very good companies will be cut from the certified list and you need to be prepared in case you lose that major client.

## Get Contracts in Place

A great way to give lenders and/or investors a sense of confidence in your business is to show them that you have contracts in place. It proves that your forecasts are based on real evidence of revenue coming to the company. Consider giving discounts to sign a long-term contract or other incentives to get your customers to sign on the dotted line.

If you can show that you have diversity in your client base, plus signed contracts with major customers, funding sources will have a sense of security, and this will facilitate the financing process. Review your customer segmentation lists in order to identify the best clients with which to build relationships and offer incentives to get long-term contracts in place.

## Customer Segmentation

Marketing 101 starts with segmentation, targeting, and positioning. Chapter 6, *Marketing Strategies and Execution*, defined customer segmentation as the division of a client base, market, or industry into discrete client or customer groups sharing similar characteristics. For example, your customer base may be men, ages 20 to 40, who are hunters interested in camping equipment or women over 50 who are interested in wrinkle prevention. The reason for this type of segmentation is to make it easier for each business to identify, select, communicate with, and appropriately service their target audiences.

Customer segmentation is a powerful mechanism to identify unmet customer needs. Companies that identify underserved segments can outperform the competition by developing uniquely appealing products and services. Effective segmentation enables your business to allocate resources to the most profitable segments and select the most effective marketing, product development, and service delivery strategies.

Financing sources want to see that you have a diversified base, understand the trends facing each of those segments, and provide customers the products and services that they want and need.

In completing an effective segmentation, you may be able to do the following:

- Identify that you have less customer or product concentration than you initially thought.

- Develop a plan to sell more to your smaller clients.

- Maximize your profitability with existing clients.

Study after study shows that if you do it effectively, your business will be successful.

Market segmentation looks at how a potential market can be divided up into smaller segments that are more efficient to serve. The same process is undertaken when analyzing your own customer base. This can then be extended out into the broader marketplace to look for potential business.

Once your client base is "sliced and diced" into specific segments, determine what products and services you have provided, are currently providing, and what others you can sell to them in the future. When you know who you are going after—as a conscious choice—you can position yourself to speak to your target audience through the channels they use.

As you begin the segmentation process, determine the various segments in which to divide them. Include the following categories:

1. Revenue

2. Market or Industry Segment

3. Demographics

4. Services/Products Purchased

5. Age of Client Relationship

6. Product/Service Usage

Segmentation is most effective when a company tailors its products and services to the specific segments that are the most profitable and provides them with distinct competitive advantages. This prioritization can assist organizations to develop successful marketing campaigns and pricing strategies to extract maximum value from both high and low-profit customers.

Follow this methodology to develop effective customer segmentation:

1. Divide each target market into meaningful and measurable segments.

   – This can be handled in a variety of ways: geographical location; size and type of organization; lifestyle, attitudes and behavior of consumers; or a host of other categories.

2. Determine the profit potential of each segment.

   – This can be done by analyzing the revenue/cost impacts of serving each segment and determining pricing strategies appropriate for each segment.

3. Target segments according to profit potential.

   – This should include the company's ability to serve this segment in a way that provides the business with a competitive advantage.

4. Effectively allocate resources.

   – This will enable the business to develop specialized product and service offerings, design marketing and distribution programs to match the needs of each target segment, and create new products and services appropriate to specific segments.

5. Measure performance.

   – This allows you to track and adjust the segmentation strategy and make effective decisions.

To summarize, the advantages to conducting a comprehensive and effective customer segmentation process can help you:

- Identify your most-profitable customers.

  - This can enable you to focus your marketing efforts on those clients who have need of your products and are most likely to buy. This will provide you with more cost-effective marketing and promotional programs by using your resources wisely.

- Determine your least-profitable customers.

  - This allows you to avoid the markets and segments that will not bring in profitable revenues.

- Improve customer service.

  - By understanding your target market, you can more easily improve your current product and/or service mix and identify new ones to meet customer needs.

- Beat the competition.

  - You will build loyal relationships with your customers by developing and offering them the products and services they want. This can allow you to get ahead of the competition in specific markets.

- Increase profits.

  - You can increase your profit potential by keeping costs down. You can also determine whether you can successfully charge a higher price for some of your products and services. This would require testing to ensure that this will be appropriate for your target market.

## You May Have More Diversity Than You Think

The manner in which you showcase your customer base will determine how the lender or investor views the level of concentration. It can also affect how you develop your marketing strategies and even the level of revenue coming into the company.

Once you understand the needs of a segment, you can implement a strategy of product differentiation to help clients and potential clients perceive your product or service as being different, and better, than the competition's offerings.

One-size-fits-all markets do not exist. For example, Procter & Gamble had different targets for each of its detergents. As the size of the middle market shrinks, P&G has a new segmentation strategy: Offer different products to reach 1) high-income and 2) low-income families. It expects this will increase sales, profit and return on investment.

Even if you have only one product, you can still develop multiple market strategies. For example, magazines are frequently directed at two or more market segments. *Sporting News Baseball Yearbook* uses 16 different covers featuring a baseball star from each of its regions in the United States.

A good example of multiple products and multiple market segments is the car industry. Ford Motor Company's different line of cars, trucks and SUVs are each targeted at a different type of customer. But having more products may not be the answer. Ford learned that, even for a company as large as it is, too many models and options can be devastating to the bottom line. In its turnaround, Ford reduced the number of models from 97 to 36.

After reviewing its lines, Ford decided to sell off the Jaguar, Land Rover and Volvo brands. By simplifying its product line, Ford made more money by offering fewer models at a lower cost. Ford could do this because having fewer models meant it had fewer basic designs to debug. That enabled the company to produce higher volumes, increase the overall quality, and significantly lower prices.

So take another look at your customer base to ensure that you have identified each of your market segments. Lenders and investors want to see diversity in your client base as well as appropriate strategies directed toward each of those market segments.

## Getting Started

Identify the segments that already exist in your client base and create service offerings that really hit the mark. Below are examples of worksheets you can use.

As previously discussed, first divide your clients by market or industry group and identify the products and services you are providing to them. The table below represents an example for a strategic marketing consulting firm.

### Client Listing By Market Group

| Client/Customer | Market Segment | Product/Service Purchased |
|---|---|---|
| Client A | Technology | Strategic Planning |
| Client B | Individual | Career Counseling |
| Client C | Professional Services | Branding, Marketing Strategy |
| Client D | Retail | Promotional Programs |

Once you have completed the identification of segments for each of your customers, create a list for each individual segment. Then create a separate worksheet for each segment you have identified (e.g., technology, retail, manufacturing, professional services, etc.). This may be helpful in identifying which clients you may have additional cross-selling opportunities in order to grow your company. But this also helps a financing source get comfortable with diversification in your business—diversification by client and by service. Since financing sources are quantitative, it is important to display this client segmentation in dollar terms, as shown in the table below.

## Market Specific Client Segmentation Worksheet

SEGMENT_____

| Client | Annual Revenues | | | | | Products & Services | |
|---|---|---|---|---|---|---|---|
| | Year 1 | Year 2 | Year 3 | Year 4 | Year 5 | Type | Revenue |
| | | | | | | | |
| | | | | | | | |
| | | | | | | | |
| | | | | | | | |
| | | | | | | | |
| | | | | | | | |
| | | | | | | | |

By conducting a customer segmentation analysis and creating a market-specific client segmentation lists, you will obtain data regarding the types of segments you represent, the products and services you are providing to each segment, and the revenue generated for each segment. This will provide you with information you need to understand how to grow customers in each segment and what additional products and services can be provided to expand that market. Your marketing strategies should be based on your client segmentation, as well as research on the trends in the industries you represent.

## Summary

In building a long-term successful business, maximizing the value of the company, and improving your ability to win financing, you want to minimize concentration. Financing sources will look at your proposal with an eye towards diversification in a variety of areas.

In evaluating the risk related to client concentration, financing sources will review the number of customers that you rely on for revenues. This is to ensure that you are not reliant on one or two clients for the bulk of your revenues. They will also look at your segmentation to determine market diversification (multiple product and service offerings) to make certain that your company will not be assaulted if something adverse happens to one of the niches that you represent. Lenders and investors want to be secure in the knowledge that your company has stability and strong potential for growth.

Develop this information to build a successful growth strategy, and present this information in an exciting manner to show that your growth potential is based in fact. Including this detail in your presentation will help you win both the hearts and minds of lenders and investors to get them to invest in your business. But most importantly, this level of research will also help you improve your business and increase the value of your company.

# Chapter 12

# Secret #5

# An Effective Dashboard Will Help Navigate You to Financing

*"...That yesterday is a canceled check,
tomorrow is a promissory note.
Today is the only cash you have; so spend it wisely."*

~ Ay Lyons

D ashboards are not just for cars! An efficient and effective dashboard can be an extraordinary help in building your business and maximizing your profitability. It assists you in determining and monitoring your key performance drivers, giving you a historical perspective of your business's essential data points and expectations of future growth.

Lenders and investors are very interested to see the drivers of your business, which include financial and sales metrics. You may already have a dashboard that you use in running your business. If you do not, this chapter will provide more information on exactly what a dashboard is and help you develop one. This is useful in improving the performance of your business and is helpful in the process of winning business financing.

Presenting your dashboard demonstrates your knowledge of your business and strengthens the perception that you are the "A" team. Your dashboard should be backed up by the financial statements of the business listed in the financial section of your presentation.

## Developing an Effective Dashboard

A dashboard is a one-page representation of your *Key Performance Indicators* (KPI) in a quantitative and/or graphical form showing current and historical trends of the organization. The dashboard is meant to help the leadership of the company make informed decisions to drive the growth and profitability of a business.

The customary components of a dashboard include last year's actual data, this year's plan, year-to-date results and forecasts for the year. Dashboards are customized to a specific organization's or a department's goals (sales, marketing, production, human resources). The overall goal is to provide you up-to-date information about the business to pinpoint areas that may be problematic or are exceeding objectives.

Each organization will have its own needs, and therefore, the dashboard should be designed to provide the information you need, in a ready-to-read format. There are many dashboard templates available for you to review. Talk with your department managers and IT people when developing a dashboard for your business.

You don't want to measure everything—just the most important items that impact your business. You should start slow and build your dashboard identifying the five to ten top Key Performance Indicators (KPIs) that are important to measure on a regular basis. These may include revenue, sales performance, customer growth and retention, employee performance goals, etc. The items to be included will depend in large part on your business plan.

Once you have defined the metrics you want to monitor, you have to consider how you want to visualize them – bar charts, line graphs, and numerical listings. The goal is make it easy to review and analyze, so it will be based on your preferences.

There are three types of dashboards: operational, strategic and analytical. An operational dashboard displays data that helps facilitate the operational side of the business. For example, in an eCommerce business, you will want to monitor statistics such as the number of unique visitors or your website's up-time and utilization for different periods (for example, the year-to-date average and the actual for the prior week).

> **Showing financial sources your dashboard will demonstrate your knowledge of the business and strengthen the perception that you are the "A" team.**

Strategic dashboards usually focus on the company's main KPIs, which the business managers track on a regular basis—daily, weekly or monthly basis. This dashboard should provide the management team an overview of the state of the business. This may include a periodic review of revenue or sales versus the prior period, or it may focus on costs or even headcount, depending upon the needs of the business.

Analytic dashboards could display both operational and strategic data, but these usually drill down to more detailed information; e.g., sales by city, state or region. Different users may require different dashboards, which can be created to assist a department or functional group; for example, the dashboard could be set up by products, which includes development and production data, or focus on financial issues, which would focus on actual and forecasted information. Dashboards are created to meet the needs of the business, a department or functional area. Some metrics and KPIs that are seen on dashboards include:

- Finance

    - Report actual sales to plan (volumes and dollars), cash flow, credit to customer, etc.

- Sales and Marketing

    - Analysis of current to past campaigns, revenue dollars per catalog, average order in dollars and units, total number of one-time buyers to multi-buyers, etc.

- Inventory Management

    - Details about initial customer fill rates compared to annual fill rates, summary of cost recovery and margin loss by liquidation, as well as coverage of products/SKUs as new catalogs are mailed.

When embarking on building a dashboard, start small and determine the most essential key performance indicators you need to monitor to ensure the company stays on plan. Set realistic benchmarks and make sure of the integrity and timeliness of the data. The dashboard can play an important role in achieving sales and profitability goals, if used effectively. Additionally, it shows financing sources that you know and are focused on the primary drivers of your business. It promotes the perception that you are an "A" management team that will succeed in the future.

## Understanding Funding Sources Requests

Though the dashboard is helpful, all financing sources will request significant additional information before deciding whether to loan money to you or invest in your business. Many business owners believe that financing sources ask for too much information. Executives are not financial experts and, therefore, may not be familiar with customary requests from financing sources. Since they don't "talk" finance, they may not understand why they need a dashboard of metrics or why they need to provide more detailed financial information.

There are three basic financial statements that funding sources want to review.

*Income Statement*

The income statement identifies the revenue, expenses and profitability of the company. In evaluating historical annual income statements, the reviewer can see the growth, stability or decline in operations of the business.

Financing sources want to see the income statement to identify how the company has performed over time with increasing revenue and managing its expenses.

*Balance Sheet*

The balance sheet identifies the assets, liabilities and equity of the company. The assets may be cash, inventory, receivables owed to you by clients, equipment and real estate. The liabilities may be amounts owed by your company to your vendors, accrued expenses related to operating the business, and debt owed by your company to a lender. The equity of the company is the amount that shareholders have invested into the company, plus or minus the cumulative net income of the company, less cumulative dividends paid to shareholders.

Financing sources want to see the balance sheet to identify the assets owned by the company, which, for example, may be used as collateral for a loan, as well as how much equity is in the business.

## Cash Flow Statement

The cash flow statement identifies the cash flow in and out of the company. This differs from the income statement in that non-cash charges (such as depreciation and amortization) are added back to get a true look at changes in cash and cash balances.

Financing sources are interested to see how much cash your company has generated and how much cash it needs to operate. A lender, for example, will be very interested to see significant cash generation over time to gain comfort that the business could repay a loan if one were provided to the company.

Financing sources will be interested to see historical financial statements for three to five years (or fewer, if your business is less than three years old) as well as projected financial statements. When they ask to see *financial projections*, they want to see the same three basic financial statements showing the performance of the business over the next three to five years.

In addition to the financials, it is helpful to provide a management discussion and analysis (MD&A) of the historical and projected results. Financing sources want to understand why the business performed in the way it did. For example, if revenue increased 50 percent two years ago and then increased 20 percent the next year, why did growth slow? They want to identify if it was a price or volume issue. Perhaps you were preparing to offer a new product and revenue is expected to return to 50 percent per year, but the lender will not know the story unless you provide it. The MD&A should explain annual changes in revenue and expenses for each of the historical years and each of the projected years. In addition to being helpful to financing sources, it is beneficial to provide commentary on the projected financials to confirm you are comfortable with the growth you expect to achieve.

When a funding source asks for an *Interim Statement*, they want to know:

- The business' income and expenses since the last tax filing.

- Any changes in the business' financial situation that would prevent repayment of the debt.

## Providing Financial Statements

Your CPA is the best source to help you create all the documentation you need to present effectively to a funding source. This information can be used to build your dashboard. When developing your presentation for a potential financing source, focus on:

*Revenue & Expense Growth*

Provide the funding source with a comprehensive, historical look at your company's revenue growth. This includes revenue information representing:

- Each month for the last 12 months.

- Each year for the last 3-5 years.
    - Or, if your company is less than 3 years old, for each year you have been in business

- Each product and service you offer.

- New products and services you have developed.

Financial projections are a very important part of your presentation to a funding source. They will determine whether you get a loan or investment into your business. As you are projecting your future growth, always keep in mind that projections are just good guesses. To gain credibility with a funding source, your projections need to be as realistic as possible. The best approach is to use your historical performance as a guide.

If you are a startup, research the market and then base your projections on the historical performance of other companies within your market segment. Your trade and professional associations may also have information on your industry for your presentation.

Take a moderate tone when making projections. The most comprehensive way—and what most funding sources really appreciate—is providing projections on worst-case, base-case (which is also what you believe to be the most likely case), and best-case scenarios.

## Cash Flow

This is the movement of money in and out of your business and is especially important to a lender. In evaluating whether to provide a loan to your company, lenders want to identify specifically how your business will be able to generate enough cash flow to repay the loan. If lenders cannot see adequate cash flow in your business, your request for a loan will be denied.

Your cash in-flow is based on the sales of your products and services. This can also include borrowed funds, interest from investments, and income from asset sales.

Cash out-flow will include such expenses as wages, purchasing inventory and raw materials, buying equipment, operating costs, repaying loans and, of course, various taxes.

Cash repays loans. So when financing sources review your presentation, they know that repayment of their loan depends on your projected cash flows. They know that all businesses can be impacted by a changing economy, differences in consumer demand, pricing and other trends. To present yourself as a sophisticated and knowledgeable business, present worst-moderate-and best-case projections.

*Ratios*

Financial professionals have their own language. In many cases, they speak in "ratios." While you don't have to become totally proficient, you need to understand the financial basics to converse effectively with funding sources.

Ratios are the financial short-hand that funding sources use to show trends and variations that can help manage the business. There are several usual and customary ratios that you should include as part of your presentation to your financing sources. Some you may be very familiar with, such as Profit Margin which shows how efficiently you are managing expenses:

$$\text{Profit Margin} = \frac{\text{Net Income}}{\text{Sales}}$$

Another ratio is Return on Investment (ROI):

$$\text{ROI} = \frac{\text{Gain from Investment} - \text{Cost of Investment}}{\text{Cost of Investment}}$$

A Current Ratio shows whether you are able to pay short-term debts:

$$\text{Current Ratio} = \frac{\text{Current Assets}}{\text{Current Liabilities}}$$

Depending on the type of business you have, you may be required to provide different ratios.

A list of usual and customary ratios and their formulas is provided in Appendix B. Review them with your CPA and determine which ratios would be necessary for your presentation.

## Summary

Don't get overwhelmed by the need that lenders and investors have for financial information and metrics. Your CPA is well versed in all these matters and will be working with you to establish all the documentation you need. If you don't have a CPA, then it is imperative that you get one. He/she can be one of your best advisors in growing your business.

# Chapter 13

# Secret #6

# Increased Profitability Can Be a Positive or a Negative

*"A business absolutely devoted to service will have only one worry about profits. They will be embarrassingly large."*

~ Henry Ford

Generally, people want to maximize profitability. It shows a successful business, it allows the business to pay higher salaries and bonuses to employees (and the owner operator), and it allows for more dividends to be paid to shareholders. Profitability also provides a sense of comfort to employees, clients, and other stakeholders about the business's success.

For companies seeking loans, maximized profitability can increase the win rate for debt financing. For companies seeking equity funding, some investors want to see historical growth in performance, but it might be through increased revenue, gross profit, pre-tax income and/or post-tax income.

Some investors who invest in growth companies would prefer to see a management team invest to maximize growth potential by developing larger sales teams and spending more on research and development. Those investors need to believe that additional growth will be there in the future, and when such extraordinary growth costs are stopped (or decline as a percent of revenue), profitability will be maximized—not necessarily today, but within three to five years.

This is seen in such examples as Groupon, Facebook and Twitter, which had high growth potential but never earned a profit when they received equity funding. Those companies did, however, have the Big Idea—disruptive technology—and had significant growth potential.

Depending upon which growth/profitability strategy you are pursuing, identify if such a strategy is in-line with the investment thesis of each financing source you are planning to meet.

## Start With Profit Goal in Mind

For most people, profitability is the difference when you subtract expenses from revenue. It is the "what's left over" that is responsible for:

- Raises

- Promotions

- Training Opportunities

- Growing the Business

- Owner's Equity

An effective business looks at profitability as a decision, not what is left over. It is what financing sources look at when evaluating your firm for credit or investment. You want to show them that you are implementing policies focused on continually increasing your company's profitability.

Benchmarking is the most effective manner to begin this process. Be in the top 25 percent of your particular industry. First, identify the benchmarks in your market. Trade associations are a great source of information that can help you set your goals. Many trade and professional organizations conduct "cost-of-doing-business" surveys that they update regularly. These groups should be able to provide you with metrics for the "average" companies in your industry, as well as those in the upper tiers.

Most research shows that average companies may generate more revenue but will have higher expenses and, therefore, lower profits. The top companies in most markets are more attuned to implementing efficient systems that lower costs and result in higher profits. Benchmarking allows you to research how the top companies do it, and you can then start implementing those processes in your own business.

As mentioned in previous chapters, funding sources look at how well your company is doing against the benchmarks in your industry. Showing financing sources that you benchmark with the top quadrant of companies in your industry will help you to win funding.

This table shows industry benchmarking metrics:

| Company Metrics (Using Industry Data) | Average Company | Top 25% Company |
|---|---|---|
| Revenue | $1, 239,262 | $937,279 |
| Expenses | 1,199,033 | 806,572 |
| Operating Profit | 40,229 | 130,707 |
| Operating Profit % | 3.8% | 12.6% |
| Owner Compensation | $80,000 | $140,000 |
| Total Owner Return | 120,229 | 270,707 |
| Total Return % | 10.8% | 26.1% |

As you can see, the top company, while generating less revenue but implementing effective systems to limit expenses, doubled their returns.

So what does it take to build a firm with increasing profitability—or the potential for high profits in the future? There are a number of tasks you can implement:

- Build and Motivate a Great Team

- Measure Key Performance Indicators

- Focus on Productivity

- Enhance Client Retention

- Provide Great Customer Service

- Increase Sales

- Improve the Product/Service Mix

- Gain Pricing Power

- Cut Unnecessary Costs

- Reduce Capital Needs

## Build and Motivate a Great Team

The most critical component of a business is its people. As discussed previously, financing sources tend to fund the best team, not necessarily the best proposal. Financing sources love to see experienced teams.

The goal is to hire the best people you can afford and give them what they need to be successful, efficient and productive. If you hire people who are not ideally suited for their roles, managers will spend too much time coaching and productivity will decline (and frustration levels will increase!). If managers can delegate to individuals who have their confidence, the team's productivity will soar.

As a general rule for small company success—the smaller the company, the more experienced the team should be. With an experienced team, you will be more productive and get results more quickly because the learning curve is shorter. This is not always the case, because many small companies cannot afford the most-talented, most-experienced professionals; however, there are benefits to combining the more experienced professionals with younger, highly-talented individuals.

Also engage your key people in developing as well as executing the business plan. Use their knowledge of the business and challenge them to create new revenue, product, and efficiency ideas. Review results regularly with their input.

> **The goal is to hire the best people you can afford and give them what they need to be successful, efficient, and productive.**

As mentioned, small businesses usually don't have the resources to hire the key staff that they need. A great way to accomplish your goals is to use contractors. It is more cost-effective than hiring full-time employees and less time-consuming than if you do it yourself. Hire these experts and delegate tasks that fall outside your expertise.

Additionally, there are organizations that will provide you with pro-bono assistance, such as SCORE (www. score.org), which provides mentors and education to help small businesses. The U.S. Small Business Administration (www.SBA.gov) also provides many courses and online resources. Also, many cities and counties offer free and low-cost programs to small and mid-sized businesses that include mentoring and education.

Do not forget to check with trade and professional organizations as well. Groups such as the National Association of Women Business Owners (www.NAWBO. org) and the American Marketing Association (www. marketingpower.com) offer educational and mentoring programs through their local chapters. Check to see what is being offered in your community.

## Measure Effectively

Renowned business authority Peter Drucker (creator of the Management by Objective strategy in 1954) said, "You cannot manage what you cannot measure."[40] Continuous measurement and feedback drives process improvement.

What measurements drive the "economic engine" of your business? Establish measurements for your key performance indicators that let you know every day how you stand in relation to your business goals. It is easier to adapt to changes as they happen, rather than waiting to the end of a campaign or program to understand your overall results. The goal is to establish systems that allow for continuous monitoring to drive positive change. Any key measurements and goals that are impactful drivers of financial performance should be included in your dashboard (covered in the prior chapter).

To measure effectively, take advantage of available technology such as good accounting software to keep track of your finances, sales, and purchases. Effective software will also allow you to keep an eye on your credit customers so that you can collect your accounts receivable in an efficient and timely fashion. Inventory software can help you take regular accountings of your products and sell off slow-moving items so they can be replaced by faster-moving ones. Use bar codes or RFID devices to keep track of your inventory and avoid pilferage either by thieving customers or your own staff.

There are numerous packages that are affordable even for the smallest of companies. The major benefit is that these programs create efficient systems, which can leverage ordinary people to produce extraordinary results. An effective system must have all the necessary components to function properly such as checklists, forms, reports, equipment, software, supplies, people, tools, and other resources. Missing or poor-quality system components are a major weakness of most small businesses.

Effective systems—in the office or in the factory—should be designed to provide the reporting you need to eliminate idle time, mistakes, unnecessary movement, inventory buildup, bottlenecks, and downtime.

You make money when your systems are reliable and provide you with the measurements you need to stay on track to meet your goals.

## Focus on Productivity

*High wages with low productivity is charity.*
*Low wages with high productivity is exploitation.*
*Low wages with low productivity is suicide.*
*High wages with high productivity is progress.*

~ Rene T. Domingo[41]

Business books and articles are filled with myriad ways to improve productivity. But it is not as simple as adjusting inputs or operating at high volumes. Productivity is finding ways of doing things smarter and better.

"World class productivity lowers total cost by focusing on minimizing the usage of inputs, not by lowering the acquisition or purchase price of inputs," states Rene

T. Domingo. She adds, "For instance, it does not justify low and exploitative wages. Japanese firms which have high productivity pay very high wages, but have low total labor costs."[42]

Productivity does not mean to become a sweat shop and push your workers until they drop. In many cases, it means augmenting workers with efficient systems and technology. By making each worker more productive, you will make more profit.

The goal of productivity is to reduce the resources needed to produce a product/service without sacrificing results by improving and streamlining the process. Companies that can continually improve their productivity can inoculate themselves from cost increases in raw materials or in wages. Then you can offer competitive prices while your less-productive competitors price themselves out of the market or become less profitable at a lower price point.

## Enhance Client Retention

The *Harvard Business Review* has stated that the average business loses 50 percent of their customers every five years.[43] Authors Emmet C. Murphy and Mark A. Murphy made several informative observations in their book, *Leading on the Edge of Chaos*.[44]

- Acquiring new customers can cost as much as five times more than satisfying and retaining current customers.

- A 2 percent increase in customer retention has the same effect as decreasing costs by 10 percent.

- Depending on the industry, reducing your customer defection rate by 5 percent can increase your profitability by 25 percent to 125 percent.

These are some impressive statistics! So what can you do with them? Ask yourself the following questions:

- How many customers have you lost in the last year? Last five years?

- How much revenue and profitability did these customers represent?

- How many customers have you gained in the last year? Last five years?

- How much revenue and profitability did these customers represent?

- What do those numbers mean to you and the success of your company? Now and in the future?

The answers to these questions can help you understand where you should be spending your marketing and customer service dollars.

Business advisors always get asked, "Which is better? Retaining current customers or adding new customers?" That is not a question that you can answer without saying, "Both are important." But statistics show that you would have an easier time increasing profitability if you retain more clients than having to replace a large number each year just to keep pace.

According to the U.S. Chamber of Commerce[45] and the White House Office of Consumer Affairs the top reasons why customers leave[46]:

- 68 percent leave because they are upset with the treatment they have received

- 14 percent are dissatisfied with the product

- 9 percent migrated to the competition

- 5 percent seek alternatives or develop other business relationships

- 3 percent move away

- 1 percent go out of business

Why do you think your clients are leaving? In many cases, what the business perceives as the reasons for a customer leaving usually does not match the reality. RightNow Technologies claims that 73 percent of customers leave because they are dissatisfied with the services provided, *but* the company thinks that only 21 percent leave for this particular reason. The company losing the customer thinks 48 percent leave because of price, when, in fact, only 25 percent do so.[47]

Not implementing a healthy client retention strategy is costing your firm significant resources. According to the Gartner Group, commitment to a superior customer experience results in up to 25 percent more retention and revenue than sales or marketing initiatives. And according to recent studies, repeat customers spend 33 percent more than new customers.[48]

What these statistics tell us is that you need to highlight customer service and find a way to manage all your customers' requests and demands in a manner that enables your company to grow profitably. Today, that means high-touch, personalized ordering and delivery systems. Identify and implement systems to get that job done quickly, effectively, efficiently, and profitably.

## Give Great Customer Service

Some 80 percent of companies believe they deliver a superior customer experience but only 8 percent of their customers agree, according to Bain & Company in a Harvard Management Update.[49]

Many businesses are unwilling to lose money on an order, even if that means ending the relationship with an unhappy or dissatisfied customer. You may have had a similar experience; you call the company and hear:

*"I'm sorry, sir. We only made $X on your purchase, so if we (fill in your reasonable request here), we'd lose money on your business. I hope you understand."*

This is a penny-wise but pound-foolish approach, and a terrible way to do business in today's highly social and connected world. If you are not consistently and pro-actively resolving customer problems, you are missing out on the chance to improve your bottom line. And with the viral nature of social media, the whole world can hear about one misstep in minutes. Cleaning up that type of mess can expend many marketing dollars that could be more effectively used elsewhere.

Unfortunately, customers today are very accustomed to mediocre service. The good news is that if your business goes out of its way to proactively resolve a problem—without charging them—you have probably secured that client for some period of time. (But, as we know, there will always be the question of, "What have you done for me lately?," so we need to keep providing great client service every day.) Apart from the lifetime value of that customer, you will receive valuable referral marketing and recommendations that are impossible to buy.

Studies show that satisfied customers tell 9 people how happy they are; dissatisfied customers tell 22 people about their bad experiences.[50] Which would you rather have?

So, what can you do to improve your customer service strategies? Mark Hayes, on the Shopify blog, listed several highly successful approaches that some eCommerce businesses have implemented.[51]

1. If a long-time customer needs something immediately, overnight it to them at no charge.

2. If an inexpensive product breaks during shipping, send a free replacement without requiring them to hassle with the return.

3. For expensive items that need to be returned, ship them a replacement as soon as they submit tracking confirmation of the return, instead of waiting until it hits your warehouse.

4. If a customer wasn't happy with a purchase, proactively issue a partial refund to help compensate for the disappointment.

These strategies build a loyal—and vocal—fan base. It may cost you extra in the short term, but you will have obtained a better brand, an incredible reputation and life-long customers that will build you a healthy bottom line over the long term.

Companies that prioritize the customer experience generate 60 percent higher profits than their competitors, according to the Gartner Group.[52]

## Increase Sales Volume

Increasing sales volume appears to be an easy way of increasing profitability, but this may not be the panacea you are hoping for. A principle to remember is that while profit does require a company to have sales, sales do not always equal profit.

Selling more of your existing products and services, or introducing new ones, may increase your sales volume. But selling more of loss-making lines is bad business—unless it is necessary in order to raise sales of profit-making ones.

The first thing is to understand the contribution that each product or service provides your bottom line. When considering increasing your sales volume, also strictly control all aspects of profitability (costs, capital, prices) as well as the product/service mix. Make sure that none of these components increase disproportionally and cause only increased sales instead of increased profit.

Many businesses believe the best way to increase sales is to boost the sales staff. The same warning applies to the addition of more sales representatives or expanding the geographic areas served. You will only make a profit if the extra salespeople produce enough extra profit—not revenue—to cover the extra costs.

Another strategy that businesses employ to generate more sales is to cut prices. But remember, you will have to create a major increase in sales volume to raise profitability. To make up for the lower sales price, you may potentially have to pay higher sales commissions (which are paid on revenue and not on profitability).

> **Approximately 80% of companies believe they deliver a superior customer experience, but only 8% of their customers agree.**

Additionally, if your sales increases come from small volume orders, this may decrease profitability because of increased administrative costs, such as invoicing and dispatching. This is doubly true if you extend credit in order to encourage more sales, causing the company to take on more costs to manage these clients, which can significantly affect your profits.

While this may seem counterintuitive, in some cases, you can increase profits by reducing sales. A disproportionate amount of cost and effort is sometimes invested to achieve a small amount of sales revenue.

The 80/20 rule shows that 20 percent of clients provide 80 percent of the revenues. In evaluating the clients to focus your efforts on first, concentrate on the top 20 percent. It is not uncommon to see that half of a firm's deliveries may account for only 15 percent or less of sales revenues. Consider selectively reducing these sales to increase your profitability.

## Improve the Product Mix

Your product mix reflects the combinations of the products or services you provide and sell to your customer base. Did your particular product mix come from careful planning and analysis or the normal pattern of a series of historical accidents? And is the mix you currently have as profitable as it could be?

The best approach to determining profitability is to examine each product in terms of its costs and the net margin it produces. Many companies find that the products producing the highest unit gross profit and contribution to sales volume are also responsible for the highest selling costs.

Do some testing to determine the best product mix for your business. You may find, for example, that you should aim to sell more of A and B, which you have found to be profitable, to supply less of C and D, which are of limited profitability, and to eliminate loss-making E and F from your sales portfolio.

An effective change in your product mix may result in decreased sales and increased profitability.

## Gain Pricing Power

Pricing is always a conundrum. Price too high and you may lose business. Price too low and your profits can decrease, and you become a commodity that will lose business to a competitor that prices for pennies less.

In a financial downturn we find businesses revert to cutting prices to increase sales. It is easily implemented, customers respond immediately, and you see an uptick (or less of a decline) in sales. You feel like you did the right thing. But price cutting can be addictive and not good for the business in the long term.

Today, all businesses need a carefully thought-out and implemented sales strategy. Pricing is fundamental to profitability. For a typical company, a one percent increase in price boosts profits by two to three times as much as a one percent increase in sales volume. Yet pricing capabilities are unknown or underdeveloped in most companies.

Real challenges cause companies to shy away from addressing pricing strategy. Customers might accept price increases if all the businesses in your market segment are part of a general price adjustment, for example, gas prices; however, raising prices in isolation without losing business requires a significant difference between your products and your competitors.

Instead of always focusing on increasing revenues, you might want to think about growing margins or improving business efficiency. As the saying goes, "It doesn't matter how much you make. It matters how much you keep."

Raising prices can be terrifying. We always assume that our customers may leave us and revenue will decline. Like most fears, the consequences are grossly exaggerated and the benefits are underestimated. A small increase in price can do miracles for your bottom line as is shown below:[53]

- Product Price:     $100
- Cost:              80
- Profit:            20

- **Profit Margin: 25% ($20 profit / $80 cost)**

By re-pricing this item at $110, the increase in margin is significantly better:

- Product Price:       $110
- Cost:                80
- Profit:              30

- **Profit Margin: 37.5% ($30 profit / $80 cost)**

A minor price increase of only 10 percent resulted in a 50 percent increase in profits and gross margin!

This pricing strategy works well when you have a strong unique selling proposition and you are not competing on price alone. In that case, your conversion rates should not decline drastically and your profits will increase significantly. Even with a considerable 30 percent drop in conversions, you would still be making more money than under your old pricing model but with fewer customer servicing costs to consider.

Before implementing any pricing strategy, it is important to test different pricing levels. While raising prices is often very effective, you will need to confirm it works for your business and in your market. An effective strategy to implement, if you offer a large number of products, is to start test pricing on only your best-selling products.

Again, remember that this strategy works best when you have a unique selling proposition and you are offering value. The more price-sensitive your customers, the less effective this strategy will be. If you do not have a unique selling proposition, develop one.

## Reduce and Recover Costs

In every financial downturn, almost everyone focuses on reducing costs to stabilize profitability. But, in many cases, businesses do this in a "penny-wise, pound-foolish" manner. Reducing business expenses is not just a matter of slashing programs indiscriminately. The goal is to develop a cost-reduction strategy that maximizes efficiency without compromising growth potential or the ability to service customer needs.

It is important to take time to consider which cuts are appropriate for your business. Analyze and target specific expenses that can be reduced, and identify any efficiencies that make each resource go further. Before you start cutting, understand what your costs really are. To do this effectively:

- Calculate your true costs by unit and total sales.

- Identify core competencies where efficiency can be improved.

- Trim and consolidate non-core functions.

- Reinvest the savings in critical business assets.

It is important to keep your employees informed as to the "why" the company needs to reduce costs and by how much. By getting buy-in from employees and asking for their help and suggestions, you will make better decisions and the implementation will be smoother.

Many companies use this time to consider outsourcing, especially for non-core business functions, such as human resources, billing, or payroll—contracting with third-party providers. Some companies have even outsourced parts of their operating processes.

Remember that outsourcing can expose your company to new risk; e.g., an inferior supplier of outsourced services can inflict permanent damage on a company's relationship with its suppliers, vendors, and customers. *This can force the company to spend major resources to clean up the mess*—money that could be better spent.

Seriously consider the impacts of specific cost reductions. Arbitrary reductions may not produce the desired results in the long term. Seek advice from your CPA, your advisors, and your board of directors.

## Reduce Capital Needs

Obtaining a good return on capital and reducing the capital tied up in your business can have a large effect on your company's profitability. Take the time to identify the categories of capital employed in your business and consider how they can be reduced. There are strategies you can implement:

- Implement Tighter Control of Credit

- Reduce Inventory Levels

- Use Technology More Effectively

A change in any category will affect other functions in the firm. Any changes evaluated must be considered in the context of all others; changes made in isolation may not have the expected impact on profitability.

## Summary

Change can be scary. Fortunately or unfortunately, we live in a time of constant change, and if we do not adapt, we will fail. You may be reluctant to try different strategies because you are not sure how it will affect your business. "If it ain't broke, don't fix it" may work for a period of time, but if we do not try new processes, we can get passed by the competition or we may be leaving dollars on the table.

# Chapter 14

# Secret #7

# Higher Barriers to Entry Means Lower Barriers to Financing

*"Scarcity creates value...By limiting choice, you can create value. Exclusivity is often underrated."*

~ Seth Godin

A dvancements in technology have made it much easier and less costly to start a business. Additionally, such developments can allow for a more level playing field for even very small businesses to compete effectively in the marketplace with the biggest players. But it is not necessarily the panacea it portends to be.

We all know how much hard work, blood, sweat and tears goes into building a business. After all that hard work, you do not want it to fail because a flood of competitors imitate your unique idea and take away your market. In addition to creating a unique selling proposition, you also need to establish barriers that will impede potential competitors from owning your space. Developing barriers for competitors to enter your space will help your business become more successful and increase its value.

Financing sources recognize the value of significant barriers to entry. Lenders and investors want to know that your business has established those barriers. Showing financing sources how your business is differentiated and how hard or expensive it would be to duplicate is important.

## Show Your Strength in the Market

Barriers to entry are anything that makes it difficult for a new entrant to break into a market. For example, an industry may require new entrants to make large investments in capital equipment, or existing firms may have earned strong customer loyalties (and put in place long-term contracts) that may be difficult for new entrants to overcome.

Barriers to entry make companies already in the market more valuable as they are subject to lower risk of new competition. We know that it is easier to get into the market in some industries other than others. For example, it is relatively easy to set up a standard online retail store. For a brick and mortar establishment, you need to find a storefront, sign a lease, commit dollars to building out the location, gain multiple permits, invest in inventory, and spend money on advertising to persuade potential customers to come to your location.

Compare that to setting up a retail online store, which requires only a website. The cost for setting up an online retailer has come down so much that the initial investment is not difficult to scrape together. While the costs of setting up an online retailer are lower, there are no barriers to entry to setting up a competing online retailer. There are, however, barriers for a similar retailer to set up a physical location near your business.

In another example, how difficult would it be for you to compete against Ford or Verizon? Setting up another competing auto manufacturer or telephone service company would be very challenging. Start-up costs would be massive, including capital expenditures for the facilities and equipment, as well as significant wage requirements for a large number of employees. And it is not just start-up money for facilities, equipment, and employees. Marketing costs would be enormous since the name recognition and branding strategies of these companies would be difficult to overcome.

Lenders and investors always look at barriers to entry in your industry. They want to see how you can overcome them in building your business, and how you can develop them to stop the competition. The ease of entry into an industry is important because it determines the likelihood that your company will face new competitors immediately. Additionally, your competitive advantage tends to disappear quickly.

On the other hand, in industries that are difficult to enter, your specific competitive advantages last longer. With that precious time available, you can develop greater operational efficiencies because of the pressure of competition. With the benefit of limited competition and potentially higher growth potential, your business will be perceived more positively by potential financing sources.

## Types of Barriers to Entry

In his landmark book *Competitive Strategy: Techniques for Analyzing Industries and Competitors,* Michael E. Porter identified six major sources of barriers to market entry[54]:

1. Economies of Scale

2. Product Differentiation

3. Capital Requirements

189

4. Switching Costs

5. Access to Channels of Distribution

6. Government Policy

*Economies of scale* is what every business wants—reduced unit costs as you increase production. If your company has already achieved economies of scale, it acts as a barrier by forcing new competitors to compete on a larger scale or be forced to compete at a cost disadvantage. If your request to a financing source is for resources to develop better economies of scale, describe how that advantage will position you more competitively in the marketplace.

*Product differentiation* is a must in today's marketplace. This can provide you with strong brand identity and customer loyalty. You can develop this through well-defined messaging in your marketing efforts, as well as in your customer-service strategies. This can be a very effective barrier to entry because it forces your competition to spend much time and money to distinguish their products from yours and overcome loyalty to your brand.

*Capital requirements* can be a huge barrier to entry if new entrants have to invest huge financial resources to compete. This can be for facilities, equipment or inventory. If the capital is needed for more risky investments, such as research and development, that can act as a strong barrier to entry.

*Switching costs* are resources expended to change from one supplier to another. High switching costs can force your competitors to provide potential customers with incentives to buy their products, resulting in higher costs. Switching costs can include retraining employees, purchasing more equipment, obtaining technical assistance and even redesigning products.

*Access to channels of distribution* can be a tough barrier to cross, if you control the main channels due to relationships you have cultivated. By controlling these avenues, you push the competition into offering sweeter incentives (price discounts, promotions and cooperative advertising) pushing their costs higher.

*Government policy* regulation can stop competitors from entering a market because of strict licensing, limits on raw materials, pollution standards, product testing regulations, and the like. If your company benefits from a government policy that limits the competition in your market, highlight that point in your discussions with potential financing sources.

But the six areas listed are not the only barriers to entry, there are many more:

- *Advertising costs* can keep competitors at bay because they cannot afford the expense. If you have an established brand, the customer may perceive your product as superior. This can make it very hard for competitors to gain consumer acceptance.

- *Control of resources* that are necessary for a company to compete can block a potential competitor from entering the market,

- *Customer loyalty* to your products can leave your competitors in the dust.

- *Distributor agreements* that are exclusive with key distributors or retailers can give you a major advantage over the competition.

- *Sunk costs* cannot be recovered if a firm decides to leave a market. Sunk costs therefore increase the risk of entry.

- *Intellectual property and patents* can provide you with the right to stop other firms from producing products for a specific period of time. *Trademarks and service marks* can also limit competitors by providing a barrier to entry.

- *Supplier agreements* that provide you with exclusive links in the supply chain can make it difficult for other manufacturers to enter an industry.

- *Tariffs* are taxes on imports that prevent foreign firms from entering the US market.

- *Zoning*, which is controlled by local governments, allows only certain activity at specific locations, which can exclude competitors.

## Understanding Barriers

Barriers to entry are not insurmountable. Many small and mid-sized businesses have the wherewithal, in terms of skills and resources, to overcome these barriers more cheaply and easily than some large companies. For example, if your product can be easily substituted for a well-branded product but can be purchased at a lower cost, you may have just overcome a major barrier.

Just as important, barriers to market entry can change over time, as an industry matures, or as a result of strategic decisions made by existing competitors. "Low entry and exit barriers reduce the risk in entering a new market and may make the opportunity more attractive financially," Glen L. Urban and Steven H. Star explained in their book *Advanced Marketing Strategy*. But "in many cases, we would be better off selecting market opportunities with high entry barriers (despite the greater risk and investment required) so that we can enjoy the advantage of fewer potential entrants."

Michael Porter classifies barriers into four general cases[55]:

- High Barrier to Entry and High Exit Barrier

    - This refers to companies in such areas as the telecommunications and energy industries

- High Barrier to Entry and Low Exit Barrier

    - Examples include national consulting and education institution markets.

- Low Barrier to Entry and High Exit Barrier

    - Hotels and ironworks fit this category.

- Low Barrier to Entry and Low Exit Barrier

    - Retail and electronic commerce fits this space.

Markets with high entry barriers have few players and thus can generate high profit margins. While markets with low entry barriers have lots of players and low profit margin.

Markets with high exit barriers are considered unstable, so the profit margins fluctuate very much over time. Markets with a low exit barrier are stable, so the profit margins do not fluctuate much over time.

When a company decides to enter a market, it has to determine how easy entering will be and how difficult leaving will be. If a market is easy to enter, many competitors will enter all the time, so the market will have strong competition. If a market is difficult for a company to leave, this also increases competition, because the company may have to take a loss to exit.

Funding sources understand these basic models, so you will need to understand where your company fits. Understanding your model, outline what barriers to entry your company has established (or will establish) and how your company can overcome barriers set up by your competitors.

## Overcome Business Barriers

Businesses have demonstrated that no matter their size, they can overcome any barrier set before them. Much of the economy's growth and innovation has come from the entrepreneurial segment. Entrepreneurs can overcome any challenge once they understand its parameters.

The strategies you can use in overcoming these barriers include:

- Differentiating Your Products

    - Conduct extensive market research to identify your ideal customer base, and truly understand why they purchase a product or service. This will allow you to create strategies that will make your product more appealing than a competitor's offering.

- Building a Strong Customer Base

    - Your research will help you determine the best ways to communicate with your ideal client. Harness the power of social media along with traditional methods appropriate for your audience. Offer incentives to other companies to help you by creating partnerships that benefit you both.

- Providing Superior Customer Service

  - Understanding your client base provides you with an advantage—you can give them what they want in the manner they want it. Make the customer experience with your company so much better than what they get elsewhere and you will have them for life.

- Doing It Better and Cheaper

  - Look for ways that you can provide your products in a more cost-effective manner. The less it costs you to do business, the more profit you will make. If you can bring down the cost of production, you can apply more resources toward marketing and branding.

- Protecting Your Ideas

  - A major entry barrier is patent and trademark protection. Patents prohibit other companies from producing the same product. If research and testing costs are very high to produce a similar product, this can prove to be prohibitive factor to competitors.

- Developing Contracts With Customers and Suppliers

  - Wherever possible, establish exclusive relationships by obtaining contracts with your customers and suppliers. With contracts, you prevent your competitors from using the same resources to compete against you.

## Essential Parts of a Business Plan

Your growth strategy should include a combination of barriers effective to keep potential competitors out of the marketplace. The best barriers exploit the strengths of your company and fit in with your business and marketing strategies. It is best to target the specific weaknesses of potential competitors; e.g., your business plan can call for a period of low prices and low profits while you focus on expanding the business. This can act as an entry barrier to potential competitors.

> **"You can focus on things that are barriers or you can focus on scaling the wall or redefining the problem."**
>
> ~ **Tim Cook**

Think about all the barriers than can be erected, which include brand strength, customer loyalty, legal constraints, qualified employees, effective pricing, lack of profitability, etc.

Look at your company's marketing strategy to see if any aspects create or increase barriers to market entry. Strategies aimed at increasing brand strength and customer loyalty will create barriers to entry.

## Summary

Once you have reached a level of success, develop strategies to deal with new companies that try to copy your achievements by entering your markets and stealing away your business. By setting up barriers to entry, you can keep the competition at bay. By limiting new entrants to your market, you can raise your prices and become highly profitable without worrying about competitors.

If you do not have high barriers in place, you will be forced to keep prices low to deter competition by keeping the market unprofitable (or with limited profitability) and not worth entering. By competing only on price, you become a commodity, and that is a tough place to be. You can never beat the Wal-Mart of your market.

The goal is to offer products and services that provide value to the client but are in some way protected from other competing products. Customers will pay for value and for great customer service; however, they will also pay for products where there is no easy substitute product. That is the space you want to play in! And that is the space in which financing sources want to invest their money.

# Chapter 15

# Secret #8

# Succession Strategies: Preparing for Disaster Can Help You Win Financing

*"Expect the best. Prepare for the worst.*
*Capitalize on what comes."*

~ Zig Ziglar

Planning for the future is an essential part of running any business. Surprisingly, only 3 percent of business owners have a business succession plan in place, according to a report conducted on behalf of U.S. Trust titled, "2011 U.S. Trust Insights on Wealth and Worth."[56] Based on the results of that study, 97 percent of business owners have not planned for an orderly transition of their business, whether as a result of retirement, illness or death.

Family businesses face unique challenges. Less than 33 percent of family businesses transition to the second generation, and just 15 percent succeed into the third, according to the U.S. Small Business Administration.[57]

Why is this important? Peak Family Business states almost "90 percent of U.S. businesses are family-owned or family-controlled companies ranging in size from small "mom-n-pop" businesses to the likes of Walmart, Ford, Mars, and Marriott. There are more than 17 million family-owned businesses in the U.S. They represent 64 percent of gross domestic product and employ 62 percent of the U.S. workforce."[58]

Most do not plan for succession, and because of that, the business might have to be sold to generate the liquid funds to pay estate taxes. Or surviving family members might have contrasting desires for what to do in the future—some may want to continue the business; others may want to "cash out" and walk away. No matter what the situation is, implementing a Business Succession Plan before a triggering event arises can help make any transition go more smoothly.

When it comes to succession planning, partial measures are not enough. Most business owners seem to recognize the importance of having a succession plan. According to a 2008 global study conducted by Prince & Associates, U.S. Trust, Campden Research, and Bank of America Private Wealth Management, some three out of four businesses consider succession planning to be an important priority.[59] Less than 40 percent of those companies, however, had actually implemented succession plans. While most business owners said that they wanted to reduce the tax burden of passing along the ownership of the family business to the next generation, more than 70 percent of those with succession plans had failed to set up effective strategies to accomplish that goal.

Adding credibility to the fact that many family-owned businesses are not prepared for succession, in a recent study by MultiFinancial Securities Corporation called, The Pulse of Practice Health[60], 18 percent of advisors to family-owned businesses said their clients had a fully documented succession plan in place and another 21 percent said they had at least a partially documented plan.

Business continuation and succession strategies are an important part of any lender or investor proposal. While many lenders and investors may make a decision to fund a company based on the strength of the management team, they also want to be confident that the business continues to function normally if a key executive leaves, dies or becomes disabled, and it is clear how the ownership of the business will change upon such an event.

## Business Continuation Planning

The success of a business may depend on the leadership and innovation provided by a key executive or a few leaders. The sudden death or disability of a key executive may have severe economic consequences, including a major loss of essential skills and abilities that are essential to the running of the business. The company may have to spend large amounts of money to recruit, hire and transition a new leader.

Additionally, key executives of the company are typically the main contacts for current clients and potential new clients. The loss of key relationships may cause a major disruption in the organization's production and sales.

Death and disability are not the only disasters that can befall the firm—the divorce of a key executive can have a major impact, too. Another consideration is the unintended consequence where the executive's spouse ends up as a partner in the business—which can be part of the divorce agreement. This is not usually a positive for the company.

What can this mean for your business? The latest statistics from the Society of Human Resource Management (SHRM)[61] indicate that the cost to recruit and train a new chief executive is typically 250 percent their annual salary. The cost to replace the owner of a small business with an annual salary of $290,300 would cost the company $725,750. Could your company survive if faced with this type of cost?

Every company needs a succession plan that includes:

- Business Continuation Planning

- Key Person Insurance

- Buy-Sell Agreements

- Sale of the Business

## Key Person Insurance

The Association of Independent Business Owners has noted that 11 percent of business owners say they are knowledgeable about the use of insurance as part of a business interruption strategy. Only 33 percent of company owners carry life insurance, however, and most of those executives carry a family life policy, not business insurance.

A more prudent strategy is to purchase life insurance on key executives. This means that the business purchases the policy on the life of the executive and pays all the premiums of the policy. The business is the owner and the beneficiary of the policy. The company must provide written notice to the executive, and the executive must give written consent to such life insurance coverage. Some businesses have even continued coverage beyond the executive's employment. If executive dies while policy in force, the business will receive death benefits income tax-free.

These benefits can help a business survive a traumatic event. The company may use the policy's death benefits to maintain operations after the executive's death. The survivors will then be faced with recruiting and transitioning a replacement. Additionally, if cash value life insurance is purchased, the:

- Policy cash value grows on a tax-deferred basis.

- Business can book the cash value of the policy as an asset on its balance sheet.

- Business may access any available cash value for emergencies or other financial needs.

Some businesses use a cash-value, key-person life insurance policy as the informal funding vehicle for a non-qualified deferred compensation plan. Talk with your financial and legal advisors before putting a plan together to understand the tax and legal implications of these types of strategies.

**Lenders May Require Additional Insurance**

Lenders may require that specific types of insurance be purchased to ensure the repayment of debt. In addition to key person insurance, you may also be required to purchase additional insurance:

- Health

- Disability

- Professional Malpractice

- Business Disruption

- Industry-Specific

Discuss the lender's requirements in detail before presenting your financing proposal. Each lender has different requirements and each business has different needs. Make sure you know what all the requirements are. Do not be surprised if a financing source inquires about your succession strategies and insurance coverage when you are making your presentation.

## Buy-Sell Agreements

A chief concern of the owners of a closely held business is what would happen to the business if one of the owners could no longer continue his/her responsibilities in running the business. There are many issues that have to be considered in this situation.

The surviving owners usually want to ensure a continuity of ownership and management without having the departing owner's successor thrust upon them. Additionally, they do not want to compromise the business by having to fund a significant buyout for the owner's successor. Business owners want their families compensated fairly for their share of the company in the event of their disability or death.

A properly drafted buy-sell agreement can achieve all of these goals by providing that:

- The owners are guaranteed that their interest in the business will be purchased, at the time of a specified "triggering event."

- The owners' interests must be sold to the company, the remaining owners, or a combination of the two.

- A specific mechanism is established to determine the purchase price based on market conditions at the time of the event.

- A funding source, through insurance policies, lenders or new equity, is established so that the liquidity needs of the business or its owners will not be onerous.

- A valuation of a deceased owner's interest in the business is established for estate tax purposes.

## Triggering Events

An integral part of any buy-sell agreement is to specify what type of situations will cause a buyout of an owner's interest by the other owners or the entity itself. As stated, the most common triggering events are:

- Death or Disability

- Desire to Sell to a Third Party

- Retirement of the Owner

- Owner's Divorce or Bankruptcy

*A death or disability* event is almost universally provided for in a buy-sell agreement. The usual terms in a buyout will include the:

- Determination of disability.

- Time for payment to the owner or the owner's estate.

- Obligation of the entity or the surviving shareholders to purchase the interest in the business.

- Funding mechanism, such as life or disability insurance, and whether it should be maintained by the entity or the owners personally.

*The desire to sell the interest to a third party* agreement should spell out the terms of any potential sale and that the other owners of the business are given the option of:

- Matching the offer made by an outsider.

- Purchasing the shares in accordance with the valuation method and payment terms provided for in the agreement.

- Allowing the company to repurchase the shares issued in accordance with the valuation method provided for within the agreement.

- Consenting to the sale by the third party.

*An owner-operator's retirement* will usually trigger a mandatory buyout in a buy-sell agreement. The conditions of such a retirement, however, can be negotiated as part of the agreement process. The remaining owner-operators would then be responsible to buy the shares of the retiring person.

In this case, the important issues will be valuation methods and payment terms. These are essential issues to iron out because, in the case of retirement, there are no outside funding sources such as life or disability insurance to help defray the costs.

*An owner's divorce or bankruptcy* is another event that can subject the business to interference from outsiders. To ensure the smooth transition within the business, the other owners of the business should have the option spelled out, which will require the affected owner to sell his or her shares to them or to sell the business itself. The buy-sell agreement should detail the payment terms and valuation methods used in this eventuality.

## Funding Upon an Owner's Death

There are a number of ways to arrange how the company will transition should an owner die. Two of the most common strategies include the *entity redemption arrangement* and *cross-purpose arrangement*. Discuss the best approach for your particular situation with your legal and financial advisors.

In an *entity redemption arrangement,* the business itself is required to purchase the owner's interest. Since this may be a huge hit to the company's liquidity, many businesses will purchase life insurance policies on each of the company's owners to cover this eventuality. The business is the beneficiary of each policy. These policies will be in an amount of an agreed-upon purchase price, which is spelled out in the buy-sell agreement.

Using this approach, the business will receive the money tax-free (if the agreement is structured appropriately). The company can then purchase the owner's interest with the proceeds from the life insurance policy. There are advantages and disadvantages to this type of arrangement depending upon your particular situation. Discuss this with legal and financial representatives.

A *cross-purchase arrangement* differs from the entity redemption because each surviving owner is personally required to purchase the interest of the owner who died. Each owner owns an insurance policy on the lives of the other owners. The proceeds would be tax-free and used to purchase the deceased owner's interest.

These arrangements can be quite complex and must be structured correctly for your company and its owners to reap the benefits. In addition, rules may differ depending upon the state requirements where your business is based. Seek the assistance of professional legal, financial, and insurance advisors to customize these programs to suit your business and each individual owner.

Executing a carefully planned buy-sell agreement can assure owners in a closely held business that their interest in the business they built is secure regardless of any unforeseen circumstances. And if structured effectively, this can be achieved without putting excessive financial strain on the business and may enable the remaining owners to keep building the business.

> **Most owners do not plan for succession; therefore, the business may have to be sold to generate the liquid funds to pay estate taxes.**

## Selling the Company

Succession issues become important, not only as you are building the company, but also when you want to sell or retire. It may be surprising to hear that seller financing is involved in 75 to 90 percent of small business sales and more than 50 percent of mid-sized company sales.

A *Wall Street Journal* article written in March, 2012,[62] stated that today, more and more sellers are asked to finance the sale of the business, and the sellers were being repaid in installments over time. In that article, Generational Equity LLC of Dallas noted that 90 percent of 2011 transactions had seller financing (typically called a seller note), compared with 25 percent of the transactions before the 2008-2009 recession. Also, they noted that sellers generally needed to finance 50 to 80 percent of the purchase price.

The reasoning is that most buyers do not have the capacity to purchase the business outright or even provide a majority of the financing. Additionally, banks may not be willing to lend to certain companies or may fund only a portion of the total purchase price. With tighter lending restrictions, many business owners are forced to provide partial, or even the majority of, financing to facilitate a deal. If you are not willing to finance at least some portion of the purchase price, you may need to consider selling at a lower valuation.

If the buyer is planning to obtain third-party funding to help finance the acquisition, you must have the bank or other lender confirm to you that the buyer is qualified. Do not spend time negotiating with a buyer who may not be able to get financing. That said, if the lender is working with the buyers, it will have an interest in providing positive feedback to support their client.

Financing a purchase almost always requires both the buyer and the seller to be involved with a lender. The buyer and the potential lender will learn as much as they can about your business before they finalize all of the deal terms. The bank wants to support their client (the buyer), but it also wants to identify how it can gain more business from your company in the future.

In this market, you need to be creative in getting a transaction completed. But there are benefits to the seller in providing some of the financing through a seller note; you can complete the deal faster and there is the opportunity to offer the sale to a larger audience by enabling more people to have access to additional funding. Additionally, you may receive a higher interest rate than with other investments and the loan will be collateralized with the assets of the business and the buyer's personal assets (though your seller note will be subordinated to the bank facility, if one is provided). Here, too, you may want to require that the buyer purchase life and disability insurance naming the seller as beneficiary until the loan is fully repaid.

The purchaser of the business also receives benefits from a seller-financed deal. There is less documentation and more flexible financing terms, and they may often get the seller to stay involved in the company providing training and/or other services to help the buyer be successful.

*If you decide to offer seller financing (partial or majority), then there are important points you need to consider.* First are taxes. You have to receive enough cash up-front at the time of the transaction to cover the taxes that you will owe upon the sale. Get an estimate as to what that amount will be, and be sure to include state and local taxes such as sales tax, stock transfer tax, or real estate stamp tax, etc., that will be due on the transaction.

Second, ensure there is enough cash, after taxes, to pay off any business loans the buyer is not assuming. Finally, determine all the other transaction costs that must be paid at closing (attorney and accountant fees, broker's commissions, appraisal fees, etc.).

> **Seller financing is involved in 75-90 percent of small business sales and more than 50 percent of mid-sized company sales.**

An additional consideration in trying to maximize the value of the buyer's bid is to allow for some portion of the bid to be in the form of an earnout, which is a future payment made to the seller based on the outcome of certain events. For example, if the buyer is having difficulty believing your projected financial performance because you expect to generate an incremental $1 million in revenue next year, you could have an earnout payment due to you in one year, if the additional revenue is actually generated.

The earnout could also be based on other financial metrics or non-financial metrics, such as the opening of a new facility or the launch of certain products. If the buyer has control of the business, there is a risk that they operate the business in such a way that they will not achieve the performance necessary for you to earn the earnout payment. Work with your financial advisor and legal counsel to develop or evaluate the appropriate earnout metric, as well as how to put protections in place to maximize the probability of your earning the additional payment.

When considering how much cash your purchaser should provide upfront, remember that many commercial lenders will require a down payment of at least 25 to 30 percent of the purchase price, to be sure that the buyer is not going to walk away if the going gets tough. This is the same requirement for you to adopt. You want to make sure that the buyer has significant skin in the game (a term financing sources always use), and should invest an appropriate amount of his or her own money in the company.

Once the sale is completed, define your after-sale role. Whether you finance the transaction or not, determine if you should stay on in an employment and/or consulting role. Define all your responsibilities when creating your employment contract and/or consulting agreement. You may also be required to sign a non-compete agreement. This will prevent you from starting a similar business in the same industry and also in a particular geographic location for a period of time. In addition to defining your after-sale role, these agreements can serve to compensate you in connection with the sale, with tax advantages to the buyer. Be sure to seek professional help when planning this approach.

## Summary

Consider a variety of issues when planning for succession. Contingency plans for operating executives must be developed to keep a company running smoothly in a time of transition.

In developing your proposal to lenders, make sure that you outline how the loan will be repaid if something happens to the key people on your management team. Such succession planning shows that you manage and plan for the future growth of the business in all situations. Make sure you have effective insurance and legal counsel, as well as financial advisory services, as you contemplate this approach.

The same strategies are appropriate when approaching investors. They want management teams that can effectively manage the company and plan for contingencies. Overall, succession planning is good for the bottom line.

# Chapter 16

# Secret #9

# Maximize Your Credit Score to Capitalize Your Ability to Win Financing

*"Let me remind you that credit is the lifeblood of business, the lifeblood of prices and jobs."*

~ Herbert Hoover

Whether you seek debt or equity, most financing sources will check your credit. Today, most lenders and investors require both personal and business credit reports from those parties applying for financing.

No matter the source, they will be looking at the "Cs" of credit to determine if you are a good risk. The "Cs" of getting financing include:

*Character*

Your integrity and trustworthiness is essential in securing financing. Funding sources invest in people not businesses, and they want to know if they are investing their money (and putting their professional reputations on the line) with a person who will "do the right thing" in all cases.

Lenders and investors want to make a profit and do not want to make a money-losing investment, but they also want to protect their reputations from being associated with bad actors or bad businesses. It benefits you to show you are one of the "good guys."

*Capacity*

Lenders want to gain comfort that the borrowers have the skill and capability to repay the money by investing the loan proceeds effectively. Equity investors want to gain comfort that the management team can create value for both the management team and the investor by growing the business.

*Credit Score*

Credit scores are important to both lenders and investors. They want to invest behind a person or a team who has been responsible with other people's money in the past. Lenders and investors understand that certain events in one's life may have been unexpected. These events could have led to a negative impact on one's credit score. If that is true in your case, do let the lender or investor know.

Some lenders have minimum thresholds and may not consider a traditional loan to a borrower who has a personal credit score under a certain level (such as 700) or a business credit score below a certain level (such as 80).

Some lenders and investors are more flexible and will invest behind someone who has a low credit score. If you or your company has a credit score on the low side, be sure to include some commentary on the reason for the low score and why they should look past that score.

*Capital*

Lenders and investors want to see that you are confident in yourself before they lend or invest money in your business or Big Idea. In addition to the significant time and effort you expect to commit to the business, financing sources want to see that you are also committing your personal wealth to it, too. Demonstrate the significant commitment you are making and specify how much you are investing.

Generally, lenders expect to see a minimum personal investment, the amount of which they use to determine the amount of the loan they will provide to your business. For example, if a lender requires a minimum personal investment of 25 percent of the loan, if you invest $25,000, the bank may provide a loan of $100,000.

Some lenders may require that your equity investment is a minimum percentage of the company's total capital structure (about 25 percent). For example, if you invest $25,000 and the bank lends you $75,000, the loan represents 75 percent of the company's capital structure and your equity is 25 percent.

Equity investors who typically invest in Big Ideas are familiar with the concept of making high-risk for high-reward investments. This type of investor may not require as much skin in the game related to your personal dollar investment, but they will also be taking an equity stake in the business and will share in the upside (whereas, a lender wants the loan repaid and earns interest on the loan, not upside).

*Cash Flow*

Cash is king, especially when you are identifying how you will repay a loan. Revenue and profitability are important metrics, but if you need to reinvest all of your cash to continue to operate or to grow the business, a lender may question how they will be repaid in the future.

It is important to show a lender that your financial projections were developed with reasonable assumptions for the repayment of the loan. In the same vein, an equity investor wants to see the same type of projecttions. They should show strong growth of the business as well as provide for future dividends and/or capital gains from their investment.

*Collateral*

Lenders know that not all loans can be repaid from the cash flow generated from a business. They recognize that unforeseen events can negatively impact any business. Lenders recognize that a variety of things in a business or in the environment can go wrong. Business owners should take steps to identify and mitigate any possible issues before approaching a lender.

Many lenders require owners to provide personal guarantees and to use their personal assets as collateral to secure the loan. In the event the loan cannot be repaid, the lender has the contractual right to come back to the business owner to use his or her personal assets to fully repay the loan.

*Conditions*

Financing sources always look at the political, economic and environmental conditions that may impact your business and how it can affect securing capital. It provides confidence to the lender or investor that they are making a wise decision to support you with financing if you can identify the most likely potential risks that could negatively impact your business and the steps to mitigate them.

## Personal Credit

Funding sources look for individuals and businesses that have good credit histories because it is an easy tool for them to use to identify which borrower is most likely to repay a future loan. It also identifies which people or businesses have been the most responsible with credit in the past. Many lenders do require a minimum level of personal credit score (recent studies with regional lenders show that the most successful borrowers have a credit score of 700+). As of June, 2013, the average personal FICO credit score in the United States was approximately 692. Scores do differ by state, and you can see a chart listing the average credit scores by state at www.credit.com.

> **58.8 percent of small businesses used business credit cards while 43.5 percent used a personal credit card for business\***

*\*63Federal Reserve System*

Today, almost all lenders are requiring both personal and business credit reports when applying for money, credit lines, loans and leases. Ask lenders if they have minimum requirements regarding business and personal credit scores. If so, find out what their minimum levels are. Additionally, ask about other relevant issues that can be used in tandem with a personal credit score, especially if you do not meet the 700+ score. Investment sources may have different needs; make sure you ask them for what they expect.

The first step is to get copies of your credit reports from all three credit bureaus—Equifax, Experian and TransUnion. By law, you can get free copies of these reports once each year as required by the Fair Credit Reporting Act (FCRA). Go to www.annualcreditreport .com to request a free copy of your credit report. Please note, that you will not get a copy of your credit score, but you will get a copy of your credit report. You will have to pay a fee to obtain your scores from each bureau.

Once you have your reports, check for inaccuracies. A February, 2013, Federal Trade Commission study of the U.S. credit reporting industry[64] looked at 3,000 credit reports and concluded up to 42 million Americans, about one in five with a credit history, have errors on their reports. The study found that for 5 percent of consumers (approximately 10 million people) those mistakes are serious enough to result in higher costs for expenses, such as insurance and car loans, and possibly stop you from getting financing for your business.

Make sure all favorable information is reported accurately. For example, all credit cards should list both your credit limit and your current balance. If the limit is not listed, it looks like you are using all the available credit on your card, which is a major red flag and will negatively affect your credit score.

If you have unfavorable information on your credit report, you have the right to minimize it by using a "Consumer Statement" which provides your statement on the particular item. The law allows you 100 words to explain each unfavorable item. Explain how you have tried to have this inaccurate information corrected. Also take the additional step of informing the potential financing source of why any potentially negative item is on your credit report. They will see it, so it benefits you to be proactive in explaining any issues.

It is your responsibility to verify with the credit bureaus that the information they report is correct. Formally dispute any inaccurate information. This can be done online with the bureaus. Once you file with the bureaus, they are required to investigate the claim. You, however, also need to personally contact creditors that are reporting inaccurate information immediately and negotiate with them to remove unfavorable entries to clean up your credit report.

Additionally, if you have opened or closed accounts that are (or were) paid in a timely fashion and are not listed on your credit report, you can request that information be added. Additional credit history can be helpful to your score as well as to showing more history of your responsible use of credit.

Check for inquiries that are listed on each report. No one is allowed to run a credit report on you without your permission. The only exceptions are the companies that hold your credit cards, as well as any lender that you have a loan with—they do have the right to check your credit. Dispute any inquiry which is not yours or is older than one year. Note that inquiries can affect your credit score.

## Business Credit

Personal and business credit have different rules. What is considered normal and acceptable for corporate credit profile, such as filing multiple applications for credit that are normal for a business, can have highly negative impact on a consumer credit profile.

Establish credit in the name of your business and build a credit history. The business credit file is based on past and current credit history of your particular company and is used by potential creditors, vendors, clients or business partners to gauge how reliable your company is and whether to extend credit or engage in business relationship. It is especially important to funding sources when approaching them for investment or loaning operating capital to your company, leasing property, supplying equipment, etc.

Business credit is important to ensure that your company has the ability to respond rapidly to market demands or growth and helps when you need to increase operations without having to "front the cash."

> **37 percent of small business relied on credit cards to meet capital needs.***

*65 National Small Business Association

Lenders base their interest rates on your business credit profile and rating for your business. Additionally, having well-established credit can provide your business with significant savings in interest rates, more favorable lease and loan terms.

It is important that you do not co-mingle personal and business credit. The conundrum here is that you may have to as you begin to build business credit. Most credit card companies want owners to be personally responsible for business debts by asking for personal guarantees. You may have to do this initially to build a good credit history for a couple of years; then ask for the personal guarantee to be removed.

Unfortunately, by providing a personal guarantee, your business credit card will appear on your personal credit report. The upside is that you will personally have more credit history; however, the downside to this is that it can make your business appear inadequately funded or operated or that the business credit is unstable or overextended.

## Creating Business Credit

Business credit cards can alleviate cash-flow crunches and makes it easier to respond to the company's needs for purchases of goods and services. It may not be the best source of capital given the high interest rates charged on outstanding balances but can be very useful when cash is tight.

Business credit cards also make it easy to track expenses and keep accurate records for tax purposes. They may also offer higher spending limits than personal cards. Additionally, they allow you to offer each of your employees credit cards with set limits. This can simplify tracking expenses and travel reimbursements. When payments are made as required, business cards will help your business build a positive credit history and put you on the road to a strong credit profile and company rating.

But, as with all good things, there are definite drawbacks to small-business credit-card usage. As noted previously, if you need to provide a personal guarantee, your personal and business finances are blended. With a personal guarantee, the business credit cards carry the same personal liability as your personal card. If the business defaults, the creditor can come after you, just as they would if you did not pay the bill for your personal credit card.

As long as the personal guarantee is in force, all will be noted on your personal credit report. The good news is that after a few years of regular, timely payments, your business will have established its own credit history. Then the credit card company may be willing to remove personal liability from the business card; however, it is your responsibility to begin the conversation to accomplish this.

Be forewarned that business credit cards have fewer consumer protections than personal credit cards. For example, if you have a dispute with billing errors or other claims, the credit-card company may not get involved or may provide less support during your defense. You will have to follow up with any issues that arise.

The following are tips on getting a business credit card:

- Register with a business credit-reporting bureau.

  - Experian, Equifax, TransUnion, Dun & Bradstreet

- Get your personal credit in order.

  - Because your business credit will be tied to personal credit, be sure that any potential negative issues related to your personal credit have been resolved. Once you have a separate business credit profile, call the credit card company and request that the credit of the business stop being reported to consumer credit bureaus.

- Secure a business credit card.

  - Start with your bank. It is usually the easiest way to get a business credit card.

  - Next, get a retail card from a supplier (Sam's Club, Home Depot, Staples, or a gasoline company).

  - You can also check bank card websites, such as, www.bankrate.com or www.cardweb.com. These sites allow you to search for business cards that offer the best deals.

Be aware of the factors that will make up your company's credit profile, such as company assets, which are the single most important measure of creditworthiness. These factors include:

- Company assets

  – What is your company worth?

  – Does your company have capital or liquid assets to effect repayment?

  – How healthy is the balance sheet?

  – How much operating capital does your company have?

- Ability

  – Can the company repay loans?

  – Were the payments made as required?

  – How much credit has been granted? By which lender and for what amount?

  – How much debt was incurred?

  – Are there outstanding or unused lines of credit?

- Acumen

  – How long has your company been in business?

  – How financially healthy is your business?

  – How is it run?

  – What type of economic environment is it operating within?

  – Is it in a declining market?

  – How is its stock performing?

- How many people does it employ?

- Are there judgments or liens against it?

- Does it readily disclose potentially negative items or business risks?

- How strong is the company's ability to stay in business?

Also be aware of what will be reviewed in developing business credit:

- Bank Account

  - The age of your bank accounts is important. Creditors will assume that you began conducting business when you opened a business checking account. The longer the relationship, the better in building the business's credit history.

- Assets

  - If the business has assets, you may have easier access to capital and credit. Some assets can be leveraged or sold for working capital. Additionally, many asset-based financing options may be available.

- Revenue

  - Your business needs to have generated revenue and must be able to show the ability to generate cash flow and manage debt. Lenders must see that the business has enough cash flow to operate normally and repay any business debts.

- Banking Ratings

    - When building business credit, you want to have an average minimum balance of at least $10,000 in your primary business checking account for the prior three months to get a good rating. The rating scale is simple: Low, Medium, High rating for the number of digits in your average bank account. If you have:

        - $1,000, your rating is "low 4"

        - $9,000, your rating is "high 4"

        - $10,000, your rating is "low 5"

To qualify for most business financing, you want to have at least a "low 5" rating. This means you have an average of minimum balance of $10,000 over the last 90 days.

Information about setting up business credit profiles with Dun & Bradstreet, Experian and Equifax is provided in Appendix C.

## Fixing Credit Problems

There are steps you can take to improve your business credit rating. First, make timely payments to companies that are rated by these agencies. Second, ensure that your repayment history is recorded in your credit profile. And third, keep your debt in check. Incur only as much debt as you need operationally. Keep tabs on all credit lines and other debt financing. Too much debt may negatively impact your credit worthiness.

Lenders base their interest rates on your business credit profile and rating for your business. As mentioned, check your credit files at least once a year, but if you have had problems listed on your report, then check them each quarter. If you need to improve your profile, consult with experts that have proven track records in this arena.

A good place to start is with the American Consumer Credit Counseling, Inc. is a non-profit 501(c) 3 organization that offers credit counseling, debt management and financial education. Please note, that many credit counseling organizations are funded by the credit card companies, and may not provide you with objective information for your particular situation. Check with your local Better Business Bureau to review a company you are considering using.

If you are dealing with bad credit issues, you can still build your business credit. Open a separate business account at your bank, and then ask them about obtaining a business credit card. Since they already have your business, they may be more likely to work with you. The bank may ask you to set up an automatic payment withdraw to make up for a less than favorable credit history.

Other options include applying for business credit card from a retail store (such as Staples) or with a company that specializes in bad credit business credit cards. You will probably get a card with low limits, high interest rates and annual fees, but it is a starting point to build better credit for better deals down the road. You can also get a secured card, where the company provides a deposit and your credit limit becomes 50 to 100 percent of that deposit.

Finally, keep your personal consumer credit profile in good standing. Although business and consumer credit files are completely different and they are not supposed to have relevance to each other unless you have provided personal guarantees.

Remember, prospective lenders or credit providers may examine the consumer credit profile of the owner(s) of your business to determine business credit worthiness. A good general rule is to actively review and maintain your personal credit file to ensure accuracy and immediately correct any inaccuracies.

## How Creditors Assess Your Business

The Business Credit Analyzer™, which is located at the end of this chapter, lists the standard pieces of information that creditors usually request. Be prepared to have comprehensive answers to each of the following items, however, if appropriate to your situation, since creditors may ask for them:

- Business Location

  - If you have a home-based business, it may be more difficult to obtain initial credit. Options include getting commercial office space to looking into executive office suites or a business incubator. Again, if you build trade credit with store credit cards, this will facilitate getting other lines of credit.

- Telephone Number

  - Certain lenders may ask whether your phone number has a directory listing. Most creditors check public records and want to see a specific business landline number.

  - Being "all cell" and using a personal cell phone number is becoming more popular for many individuals and businesses, but some creditors may view it as a positive that there is a separate, directory-listed number for the business.

- Company Website

  – If you do not have a website, put one up today. It builds visibility and credibility for your business. Not only should this be helpful for speaking with possible financing sources, but it should also be helpful in your conversations with potential customers, vendors, and employees.

- Age of Business

  – Certain lenders may have requirements for the minimum age of a company they will lend money. For example, some lenders may not offer credit to businesses less than 2 or 3 years old. They have such a requirement because they want to lend to a business that has survived through the most difficult early-stage period.

  – If you were a sole proprietor before becoming an LLC, or a C corporation, or an S corporation, use the entire period as your business age, but be sure to note how you calculated the age (so the lender does not think you are lying in your application).

  – Equity investors are less conservative and generally do not have a minimum age threshold for investing in a business.

- Number of Employees

  – If you are sole proprietor or have few employees, ask your "advisory group" if you can add them to enhance the firm's credibility.

- Also ask your attorney, accountant, insurance agent, and other professionals that work with your firm. While they may not be "employees," they can be counted as advisors or counselors to your business.

- Historical and Projected Financial Information

  - Generally, financing sources will want to see as much historical financial information as possible; however, providing three to five years of historical information is usual and customary. Both lenders and investors also want to see your projected financial information for the next three to five years. If you are a new business, you will be required to provide your business plan.

- Corporate Structure

  - It can be difficult to get credit as a sole proprietor. Consider incorporating or becoming an S Corporation or an LLC. Talk to your attorney and your CPA before making any changes.

- Federal EIN

  - This number is obtained from the Internal Revenue Service (IRS) for use on your federal taxes and for identifying purposes only. You will likely need one for banking purposes.

- Business Licenses

  - Credit bureaus check public records to verify your information. Business licenses will validate the information you provide them. Also, check with your local and state government to understand your specific requirements.

- DUNS Number

  - This is obtained from Dun & Bradstreet (D&B) and is a critical component in building your business credit history. Confirm that all information in your credit file is accurate before applying for credit.

- Paydex Score

  - If you have a DUNS number, you may already have a Paydex score. Contact D&B to get your credit report.

- Credit Accounts

  - With accounts that you have with suppliers, stores or vendors, make sure they report your payment history to D&B. Make sure that D&B provides your credit history of repayment.

- Banking Information

  - If you currently do not have a separate business account, it is imperative to set one up immediately. Remember, you should not comingle personal and business funds.

- Credit Request

  - State the amount you are requesting. Usually, the higher the amount, the more documentation you will be asked to provide. Depending upon the credit source, you may need to present some financial documentation. This may include a financial statement, several years of tax returns or even business bank statements for the past three years of the company's operations.

- Type of Credit Request

  - The type of credit (line of credit, mortgage, and lease) will determine what additional documentation you have to present.

## Summary

Many financing sources will review both your personal and business credit reports. Take the time to get copies of these reports. Examine each for errors and inaccuracies. Take the time to clean up any problems before you approach a funding source. It benefits you greatly to make sure that your credit history is correct.

Understanding how to analyze your business credit can be challenging. To assist you in this process, a Business Credit Analyzer is provided on the next page.

# Business Credit Analyzer

| Company Information | Answer | Yes | No | Pending | Additional Information |
|---|---|---|---|---|---|
| Company name | | | | | |
| Business address | | | | | |
| Is this a home office? | | | | | |
| Telephone number (listed in telephone directory?) | | | | | |
| Company website | | | | | |
| Years in business | | | | | |
| Number of employees | | | | | |
| Annual revenues | | | | | |
| Business structure | | | | | |
| Federal EIN | | | | | |
| Business licenses (city, county, state, trade and professional) | | | | | |
| DUNS number | | | | | |
| Paydex score | | | | | |
| Vendor, supplier, store, gasoline credit accounts list: | | | | | |
| Business bank (checking acct, savings, other) | | | | | |
| Amount of credit requested | | | | | |
| Type of credit requested | | | | | |

# Chapter 17

# Secret #10

# Personal Guarantees and Collateral

*"No man's credit is as good as his money."*

~ John Dewey

F inancial institutions have many options for how they invest their money. For example, they could invest in bonds, another way for them to lend money. Bonds are issued by the U.S. government, the governments of other nations, or the largest corporations in the world. These are generally considered safe investments, depending on the credit of the specific entity. Lenders could also lend money to commercial and industrial real estate or residential home buyers, which also carries risk but provides for tangible assets as collateral.

For most banks, loans to small businesses are generally considered to be on the highest-risk spectrum of potential investments. With the additional number of regulations that were created after the 2008-2009 financial downturn, there is even less interest to provide loans to smaller and riskier businesses. While loans to large companies may be readily available, there is generally a much tighter credit market for small ones.

To mitigate their risk, banks frequently ask loan applicants to sign personal guarantees before a loan request is granted. As a protection against loss, banks may also ask for you to provide collateral as a guarantee of repayment. In addition, lenders expect that you have skin in the game, and that you invest or commit your personal wealth for 10 to 30 percent of the money needed. In other words, if you need $100,000 for a project, a lender may require you to personally invest $30,000 and then provide a personal guarantee for the bank to lend your business the other $70,000.

## What is a Personal Guarantee?

A personal guarantee is very much like a prenuptial agreement. While neither party wants to think about a divorce at the beginning stage of a relationship, both parties need to determine what will happen in the worst-case scenario. The reality is that business failures are common, so the risk of a worst-case scenario must be taken into consideration.

If your lender requires a personal guarantee as part of the loan process, you will fill out a standard loan form that is a section of the loan agreement. The question will require a simple yes or no and ask for the amount that you will have to guarantee.

The personal guarantee allows the lender to take possession of your personal assets and sell them in order to repay the loan, but only if the business is unable to repay it. Depending upon the terms negotiated in your agreement, personal guarantees enable the lender or financial institution to go after your personal assets directly, even before the business assets of your company are liquidated.

Many business owners believe that their corporate structure (LLC, S-Corp, etc.) protects their personal property by separating it from their business assets. That is generally true, but not in the event you sign a personal guarantee, which is written to allow the lender to access your personal property to satisfy the debt.

The U.S. Small Business Administration encourages financial institutions to provide loans to small companies by providing a partial guarantee to the lender in the event the small business cannot repay the loan. While the SBA may provide the bank with a guarantee, the SBA wants to make sure that the business owner also has skin in the game. The SBA does this by requiring that all loans guaranteed by the SBA also have a personal guarantee from all owners of the business who hold a 20 percent or greater stake.[66] Most lenders have the same requirements for small business loans.

Let me follow up on one point above. If you own only 20 percent of a business, you may need to sign a personal guarantee, which means that in the event of a worst-case scenario, you could be on the hook for 100 percent of the loan repayment. Lenders do not always allow for a partial owner to be liable only for a partial percentage of the loan.

> **The SBA requires that all loans guaranteed by the agency have a personal guarantee from all owners of the business who have a 20 percent or greater stake.**

This can be a risky proposition for any business owner. It does not matter whether you are a 100-percent owner or a 20 percent owner. Ask yourself whether you can fulfill the pledge without significantly affecting your personal life. While all entrepreneurs understand that you can lose money in running the business, give full consideration to the prospect that in the event of a worst-case scenario, you must be prepared for the downside if you provide a personal guarantee.

Evaluate what the "worst-case scenario" means. Does it mean that you could lose your home, your retirement savings, or your savings for your child's college fund if your business cannot repay the loan and the bank comes after your personal assets? That may be the case, but give strong consideration to whether you are ready for it, and if so, identify how you can limit your exposure. You should have an open discussion with your spouse as well as your legal and financial advisors before providing the personal guarantee.

You can negotiate the terms of a personal guarantee to protect yourself. Many businesses today seek out community banks rather than banking behemoths to obtain more flexible term arrangements. Community banks focus on the small business niche and may have more incentive to make a deal work. No matter which financial institution you approach, understand that they will put your business, and potentially your personal accounts, under the microscope.

## What Is Collateral?

The SBA defines collateral as "an additional form of security which can be used to assure a lender that you have a second source of loan repayment."[67] Collateral can take many forms, but most commonly it is real property, such as your home. But it can also include:

- Accounts Receivable
  - If you bill clients for your services and have a significant amount in your accounts receivable, you may be able to use that as collateral

for a loan. Your lender will request a comprehensive balance sheet and past sales records to back up your calculations.

- Business Inventory

    - The inventory for your business can also be used for collateral. The value of this inventory can be calculated towards the business loan.

- Cash or Deposits

    - Using cash, CDs or other financial accounts are low-risk collateral for a bank. The advantage of using these instruments is that you may be offered a lower interest rate because it is a secured loan if you agree to maintain the same amount of dollars in the account as are outstanding for the loan.

- Equipment

    - Manufacturing and production equipment, computers, and copy machines can be used as collateral.

- Facilities

    - Any equity you have in your building or warehouses (or your home), or the full value if you own it outright, can be used as collateral.

- Vehicles

    - Business and/or personal vehicles can be used as collateral if there are no liens on any of the vehicles and you have clear title.

## Understanding Value

Valuing collateral is looked at differently by the lender and the business owners. The most common issue that faces businesses is that they believe the collateral they offer is worth more than it actually is. Banks are highly conservative on valuations, because if the business does default, then lenders have to take the asset, find a buyer and sell it, which expends many resources and generally leads to a lower value in a sale as buyers know banks are motivated sellers.

Generally, businesses may look at the original purchase price of the asset (which may be reduced for depreciation of the asset based on age and use), while bankers look at the current value in the market today. This is further discounted for conservatism. It may be worthwhile for you to find an independent appraiser to give you an idea of what a bank may value your particular collateral items. Get the appraisal in writing and include it in your package to the bank to provide support for your valuation.

An important issue for every business is to keep detailed records of each asset's worth on your balance sheets. When banks review financials, they will then see all the relevant data when making their evaluation.

> *The value of each type of collateral is looked at very differently by the lender and the business owner(s). The lender may give a lower value than you attribute to it.*

Another point to keep in mind is that there are two types of collateral: assets you own and assets on which you still have a loan. If you own your car free and clear, that will be viewed as a more attractive asset for collateral. If you still owe money on your home, but you have some amount of equity (based on current prices), the bank will be able to refinance that loan and claim the title. But that is a more difficult process for a lender, and therefore, less attractive.

Also, in terms of valuation, most lenders will not provide the full value to the amount of collateral. For example, most banks will value your accounts receivable at 75 to 85 percent of the value for those accounts that are less than 30 days past due and only 50 to 65 percent of the value of those accounts less than 90 days. Many lenders will not use accounts receivable over 90 days. This is another reason why you must be vigilant in your collection in advance of starting this process.

> **Some lenders may want you to back the loan 100 percent with a combination of cash guarantees and collateral.**

Use the chart below to calculate the value of your assets in bankers' terms. Note that specific lenders may have differing valuations for particular assets.

## Collateral Valuation Chart

| Collateral Type | Actual Value | Value Bank Allows | Collateral Value | Value SBA Allows | Collateral Value |
|---|---|---|---|---|---|
| Accounts Receivable | | 75-85% of Balance < 30 days<br><br>50-65% of balance < 90 days<br><br>0% of Balance > 90 days | | 75% of Balance < 90 days<br><br>50% of Balance > 90 days | |
| Certificates of Deposit | | 100% of CD | | 100% of CD | |

| Collateral Type | Actual Value | Value Allowable by Bank | Collateral Value | Value Allowable by SBA | Collateral Value |
|---|---|---|---|---|---|
| Furniture/ Fixtures | | 50% of depreciated Value | | 50% of depreciated Value | |
| Real Estate | | 75% of FMV *Minus* Mortgage Balance | | 80% FMV *Minus* Mortgage Balance | |
| Trucks/ Heavy Equipment | | 50% of Depreciated Value | | 50% of Depreciated Value | |
| Stocks/ Bonds | | 50%-90% of Portfolio Value | | 50%-90% of Portfolio Value | |
| Other | | | | | |

## How Much Should You Risk?

Before you fill out any loan application, determine what you can afford to risk. As stated, some banks may want you to back the loan 100 percent with a combination of cash guarantees and collateral. This can include per-sonal and business cash, investments and property.

Each institution has its own requirements as to the percentage of personal guarantee that is required. This information should be gathered as part of your lender comparison, which we discussed in Chapter 2. Once you understand what lenders expect, you can determine your strategy.

You want to get the best personal guarantee possible for your situation. Use your legal and financial advisors (and it may be wise to include your spouse in these conversations) to help you determine what is appropriate for both you and for your company. Your CPA can help you evaluate the:

- Extent of risk you are comfortable with before talking with a lender.

- Current value of the business.

- Liquidation value of the company.

Additionally, your financial advisor can help you determine alternative loan structures that can limit your personal guarantees. These may include collateral, a higher interest rate, a smaller loan amount or a shorter maturity period. It is important to determine what is right for you before you apply for money.

When offering personal guarantees and collateral for a loan, it is important to understand that you will forfeit these assets if your business defaults on the loan. Therefore, you should be very careful about putting up anything that you cannot afford to lose—such as your house. At least recognize the risk you are taking before you enter into the loan.

## Negotiating Terms

Lenders will evaluate all of your collateral when determining the amount they will lend to you; however, there are some key variables that they look at when setting the terms for your loan. These include how long you have been in business, the size of your company, and the performance of the organization. Your historical financial performance is a very important factor in the bank's evaluation process.

Before filing any applications, it is important to identify why a lender is requiring a personal guarantee and at what point would they no longer require one. This will help you in negotiating all the terms of the agreement. Your financial advisor can help you nego-tiate options which might include:

- Release based on the percentage of the loan repaid.

- Reduction based on business performance improvement.

- Guarantees that decrease over time.

If the business has multiple partners, the negotiation should lay out whether a joint guarantee is appropriate or if specific limitations for each partner would be better. While it is preferable not to have spouse co-sign the agreement, unless you have sufficient assets indivi-dually to cover the guarantee, many lenders may require that they do so.

Another strategy to consider is to use insurance (per-sonal guarantee insurance) to protect against personal asset loss when a personal guarantee is called in. Talk to your financial and insurance advisors to see if this is possible and appropriate for you and your business.

Dealing with personal guarantees upfront can save you much frustration—and devastating losses—down the road. Do not be bullied into accepting terms that are not appropriate for you or would be disastrous if you should have to default.

Be very clear on what you can offer before applying for the loan and negotiate with the lender until you can both reach an agreement that makes you happy. If it does not work out, you can always refuse a lender's offer and try another bank. Another option is to work with multiple lenders at one time to create a competitive dynamic. If Bank #1 requires a large personal guarantee but offers a lower interest rate and origination fee, and Bank #2 requires only a partial guarantee, but a higher interest rate and origination fee, use that leverage to win the best terms from each of the lenders to benefit you and your business.

## Summary

Using your personal assets as collateral is risky, but as an entrepreneur, you knew you were going to take risks in order to earn significant rewards with success. It is important to be knowledgeable and prepared for this process. Understand what level of risk you are comfortable with, and consult with your advisors to determine the best strategy for you and your company's situation. Shop lenders and create a competitive dynamic to secure the best rates and terms.

Be realistic about your company's needs and identify specifically how the company will be using the funds. Balance that against the risks of pledging personal assets and making a personal guarantee. If you have a history of good business credit, it will make the process of getting a loan with reasonable terms much easier. Remember that you can always turn down a lender's offer if it is not good for your business, and you can always approach another bank.

# Chapter 18

# Getting It All Together

*"The results you achieve will be in
direct proportion to the effort you apply."*

~ Denis Waitley

W hen approaching a financing source, you need to be prepared—really, really prepared. Henry Ford, the amazing entrepreneur who built Ford Motor Company, said, "Before everything else, getting ready is the secret to success." When preparing to meet with a potential financing source, be prepared to discuss many topics, not only the amount of money you are seeking and why you need it, but also any and every question about your background, your management team's backgrounds, your knowledge of the market, your secret sauce for beating the competition, and your plan to mitigate risks. In short, be ready to have your company looked at under a microscope.

To obtain a loan or secure an investment in your business, you will need to develop a well-written proposal and prepare an exciting oral presentation. I want to reiterate that this needs to be treated as the most important Request for Proposal (RFP) your business will ever do. As stated many times throughout this text, this is selling in its highest form!

Focus on the details that will make your presentation sizzle, prompting your funding sources to want to learn more. Always remember that lenders and investors are people who need to be motivated to take action—in this case to "buy" through investing in your business. To successfully accomplish this you will need to:

- Develop a written proposal, which will include:

  – Your business plan

  – All documentation required to provide a loan or make an equity investment

  – Important points (see the Success Factor Checklist in Chapter 5), including:

    • Showcasing management's skills and successes

    • Describing how this request will grow the company and make money

    • Detailing the business opportunities available in your market

    • Displaying customer diversity

    • Demonstrating effective systems

    • Exhibiting your profitability strategy

    • Outlining your barriers to entry

    • Presenting succession strategies

    • Showing your good credit

    • Confirming your collateral and personal guarantees

- Present documentation that is accurate and complete.

  - Meet all lender and investor needs and requirements.

  - Ensure all required applications are fully completed.

- Prepare an oral presentation.

  - Use an outline of your written proposal to create a short PowerPoint presentation (10-20 slides).

  - Ensure that the most critical pieces of information are included.

  - Make it sizzle!

## Preparing Your Oral Presentation

Be clear and to the point in both your written and oral presentations. The goal is to persuade your audience that your business opportunity is worthy of a more detailed look. You may get only once chance in front of the funding source when you are seeking financing for your business.

Remember that each potential financing source has many other relationships that may be helpful to you. You are not only going for a "yes" or "no" related to your financing, you may also receive valuable introductions from a financing source to other future investors and potentially to a future customer. Present yourself and your business well, and maximize your chances to win another supporter of your business (even if they do not invest).

You may only get 10 to 20 minutes to make your oral pitch. Keep the following points in mind when developing your presentation:

- Tell your story.

  - The problem

  - Your solution

- Show profit potential by describing your business model.

  - Show them how you will make money

  - Describe its growth over time

- Describe the magic.

  - Patents, trademarks

  - Specialized knowledge

  - Your unique value proposition

  - Your barriers to entry

- Detail your marketing and sales strategies.

  - Go-to-market strategy

  - What you do better than the competition

- Showcase the management team.

  - How they were successful before

  - How they will be successful again in growing this business

- Close the deal.

  - Review the problem and how your product solves that issue and how important it is in the marketplace.

- Articulate your unique selling proposition.

- Focus on the skills and dedication of the team and their likelihood of success.

- Close the deal—ASK FOR THE MONEY.

## Impressing the Financing Source

There are several issues to keep in mind when preparing your presentation:

- Your research and financial date must be up-to-date, accurate, and complete.

  - Be truthful and make it persuasive and exciting.

- Many investors make their decisions based on the team because they want to invest behind experts.

  - Highlight the skills and track records of the management team.

  - Demonstrate why you are the leaders in the field (or in the geography).

  - Make sure that you detail each members' capabilities and successes.

- Be prepared to answer the difficult questions.

  - Your assumptions and projections are good guesses.

    - Show how flexible you can be to respond to changing markets and customer demands and trends.

    - State the major risks accurately and detail how you can mitigate them.

## Make It Look and Sound Great

Hire professional help if you do not have the skills in-house, such as great writing and graphic design expertise. Your written presentation allows you to provide lots of detail in the report as well as in the appendix. Remember that your oral presentation is an overview of the major points.

Following are the important objectives of your oral presentation:

- Create a PowerPoint template that is easy to read yet dynamic.

  - Don't clutter-up the slides—less is more.

    - Make each font at least 20 points—No small text.

    - Use keywords and phrases.

    - Do not use jargon/acronyms unless you clearly define them in the beginning of the presentation to minimize confusion).

    - No more than four bullets per page. One line per bullet.

  - Think of it as an outline to your oral presentation.

- Time your presentation to meet the reviewers' time limits.

  - A 10-12-minute presentation may have 5 - 8 slides.

  - A 20-minute presentation may have 10 -12 slides.

- Do not read the slide to the reviewers.

    - Put the most important info on each page.

    - Practice talking around the keywords.

- Practice your close.

    - Asking for the money—the prime reason you are there.

    - It is all about closing the deal with a persuasive conclusion.

- Make copies of the slides for the participants.

    - This allows the reviewers to place notes on each slide.

    - They can review at their leisure.

- Be enthusiastic and confident.

    - Make eye contact with each person.

    - Smile when presenting.

- Make sure you look professional.

    - Dress for the type of person or institution you are addressing.

    - This is not the time to show your eccentricity or uniqueness. The only exception is if you are dressing to match the brand.

- Brings lots of business cards.

    - Provide to each participant.

    - Include with your portfolio.

## Practice All Aspects

The old adage "practice makes perfect" is the mantra you should implement. Rehearse, rehearse and rehearse again. In addition:

- Make sure all critical points are covered.

    - Ensure that your PowerPoint and printed material contains all the important points you want presented.

- Use a third party to give you feedback on content and presentation.

- Do a full dress rehearsal.

    - Practice until you feel comfortable.

    - Check for problems or issues.

- Videotape the presentation.

    - It allows you to see what others will see.

    - Word of Caution: Many people do not like seeing themselves on screen.

        - If you are not a professional presenter, do not be hard on yourself. The main goal is to get the financing sources excited about you and the business.

- The goal is not memorization. It is to:

    - Make you comfortable with the material and information.

    - Increase your ability to answer any questions or unforeseen events.

## Develop Answers to the Difficult Questions

Make a list of all the hard and difficult questions that can come up—they WILL!

- Prepare answers for each question.

- Practice your answers until it feels natural.

- Practice pauses before you answer questions—gives time to collect your thoughts (and avoid the "um, um, um," which never looks good).

- Be confident and energizing—don't oversell or lie.

## Present Testimonials

It is important to let lenders and investors know that your business, products and services are loved, prized, appreciated and respected.  Obtain testimonials from:

- Customers.

- Suppliers.

- Referral sources (attorneys, trade groups, etc.).

## Never Lie or Hide

Not being truthful may ruin your credibility and your request can be denied (and some financial sources may tell their network to avoid working with you).

- If specific problems may relate to the repayment of the loan, you must reveal them to lenders.

- If there are critical issues that will impact the business you need to inform your investors.

## Be Careful of What You Say

This holds true both during the actual presentation or any meeting with a lender or investor. Keep the following in mind when in meetings with financing sources:

- Talk about solutions you provide. Always speak positively.

  - Do not use the word "problem" unless you are discussing the problem you solve in the marketplace.

  - Lenders have enough problem loans in their portfolio. If they think you will be a problem, your request will be denied.

- Do not talk about anything that does not directly relate to the loan (or its repayment) or the investment in your business.

- Do not proactively bring up personal matters.

  - Be prepared to answer important questions that may relate to business matters, such as the ownership or management of the company, or your future retirement.

- Always speak positively about every employee.

  - Do not disparage or criticize any current or former employees.

  - Do not gossip (such as, employee drinking, partner marital problems).

- Do not discuss anything that is NOT a fact.

  - For example, rumors concerning changes in government regulation.

- Be very careful using humor—it can backfire.

  - Do not use a prepared joke. This is not an after-dinner speaking engagement.

  - If you are naturally funny (only in a G-rated manner), let them see your personality. Avoid potentially inappropriate or off-color humor.

## Create Checklists

Begin with creating lists for what you need to develop for your written and oral presentations. Below are some suggestions for your checklist:

*Presentation*

- Graphics

- Template

- Introduction

- Market Need

- Company History

- Product/Service

- Competition

- Intellectual Property

- Marketing and Sales

- Management Team

- Financials

- Sources and Uses of Money

- Summary

*Proposal*

- Cover Letter

- Business Plan

- Resumes of Management Team and Key Staff

- Business Financial Statements

- Proposed Uses of Funds

- List of Collateral

- List of Assets and Debts of the Company

- Listing of Receivables and Payables

- Equity Investment of Owners and Officers

- Personal Financial Statements of All Owners, Officers, Partners (if it is a requirement, such as in SBA loans)

- Appendix (research reports, marketing materials)

**Important Details**

With all the key items to create and refine, do not overlook the "important" details, such as the following:

- Confirm the meeting date and time in writing.

  – Reconfirm a day or two before the date.

- Know how much time you have.

  - Make sure your presentation does not go over the allotted time.

- Know where you are going.

  - Drive there before the meeting to know the exact location, parking, and time to get there.

- Know how to work the equipment.

  - If you are using a PowerPoint, practice hooking up the projector, etc.

  - Make certain you have everything you need (screen, internet, sound system etc.).

- Make sure you have a positive attitude.

  - All parties want to have a productive meeting.

  - Tough questions do not mean you have a hostile audience.

    - They want to make sure they are making a good deal—they have as much on the line as you do.

- Make sure you know all the names of the people to be at the presentation.

  - Practice their names. If uncommon, ask the receptionist or secretary how to spell and pronounce.

## How to Beat the Odds

Give yourself every advantage. One easy way to do that is to understand why a lender or investor may decline a proposal and ensure that you have covered all those bases. Review the following list, which outlines the usual and customary reasons financing sources have told us why they decline requests. Then prepare yourself to overcome each of these issues.

- Presenter is not Prepared

  - Documentation is incomplete.

  - Lender's application process not followed.

- Purpose of Loan/Investment does not Meet Lender or Investor Guidelines

  - Do your research, thoroughly understand each financing source's guidelines before requesting funding.

- Lender/Investor does not Service That Market

  - Again, do your research. If they state they do not service a particular area they are not going to change their criteria just for you.

- Credit File Too Thin

  - Not enough trade or business credit for the lender or investor to see repayment history.

- Not Enough "Skin in the Game"

  - Owners have not invested enough personal cash into the business to meet lender or investor requirements.

- Cannot Repay Loan

  - Owners have not demonstrated that the business has enough resources to repay the debt without strain.

- Insufficient Collateral

    - The assets to secure the loan cannot cover the debt repayment if you default.

- Bankruptcy

    - If you have filed chapter 7, 13, or 11 debt protections, lenders may deny your loan request.

    - If you have extenuating situations, (e.g., medical emergencies), discuss them with the financing sources BEFORE you file your request.

- Bad Credit

    - If your personal credit can be improved, take the time to repair it *before* applying for a loan. Correct all inaccuracies and detail extenuating circumstances.

    - Check your credit file with all three credit bureaus to ensure all information is correct.

    - If you have unpreventable issues (job loss, divorce) discuss them with your financing sources before requesting a loan.

    - If your personal/business demonstrates a bad repayment history, your loan request may be denied if you do not provide significant detail as to why.

    - You can get a loan with questionable credit.

    - Lenders may accept an explanation letter with your credit report proving that your financials have improved and describing concisely how you will repay the loan.

## If You Did Everything Right and Still Get a NO

First, obtain a detailed explanation why it was denied. If you have built a relationship with your lender before requesting a loan, they should be amenable to discussing how you can fix those issues as well as when you can request financing again. The same holds true if you have a relationship with your investors. Always explore new strategies, such as:

- Discuss ideas on how you can improve your application that will make it more acceptable to them (e.g., financial or production changes).

- Applying for another type of loan or credit (if approaching lenders) or pledging more collateral or using a third party guarantee.

- Reapplying when the timing is better for your business, especially if your industry is struggling under an unforeseen crisis.

- Reapplying when the lender or investor may have more funds to lend or invest.

### Summary

If you truly understand a financing source's requirements and exceed their expectations, you most probably will obtain the financing you need. By understanding why a funding source may turn-down a proposal and ensuring that you have dealt with each issue before presenting your financing request, you will be very well positioned relative to the other companies trying to get funding who do not know the process to maximize their opportunity for success.

Also, remember that a "No" might actually mean "not right now," and not necessarily a final no. Sometimes a turn-down is not necessarily a problem with you, which is why you need to discuss a turn-down in detail with your financing source. Additionally, as discussed earlier in this chapter, remember that each financing source has a network that might be very helpful to you in building your company. Regardless of the outcome, treat the financing source respectfully and impress them in every interaction. They may be able to help you in other ways. Not many companies recognize the value of the network of the potential financing source, and you will also stand out positively if they see how action-oriented you are in building your business.

*"Go the extra mile. It's never crowded."*

~ Unknown

# Chapter 19

# Alternative Financing Options

*"There are many paths to the top of the mountain,*
*But the view is always the same."*

~ Chinese Proverb

So what can you do if traditional bank lenders and traditional institutional equity investors are not willing to put money in your business? Seems that you can get anything online, and funding is the newest entry. Here are some alternative ideas:

**Peer-to-Peer (P2P) Lending** is a basic model of people lending money to people. It is way to bypass banks and middlemen. This is an innovative approach for someone who needs to raise money. They can go directly to people who will provide the necessary capital and is generally meant for smaller loans, typically under $35,000.

As with any channel, this is not a panacea and it has its advantages and drawbacks, as well as specific requirements that you must meet. The two main P2P programs are Prosper.com and LendingClub.com. Simon Cunningham from LendingMemo has written an overview of P2P lending and appropriate resources for you to review. It can be found at http://www.lending memo.com/p2p-lending-sites/.[68]

**Crowdfunding** has expanded from donation to lending and more recently to equity investment in small businesses. The two most well-known crowdfunding sites are Kickstarter (www.kickstarter.com) and Indie GoGo (www.indiegogo.com). The April 2012 Crowdfunding Industry Report estimates that 452 crowd-funding platforms (CFPs) raised nearly $1.5 billion in 2011, and nearly doubled to approximately $2.8 billion in 2012[69] and is projected to grow to $5.1 billion in 2013.[70]

What's more, of the four crowdfunding segments the report tracks (crowdfunded equity, lending, rewards, and donations), equity-based crowdsourcing is growing the fastest, up 114 percent this year. This amount pales in comparison to the $282 billion that American banks lent (for loans without real estate as collateral) to small businesses in 2011, according to the FDIC.[71]

With crowdfunding, a person with a business or a project that needs money lists on a site and looks for private funders. For the normal donation type of crowdfunding, the money provider does not get repaid with cash but may be offered some type of reward ranging from a personal thank you on their website to a travel reward. Generally, the rewards are related to the operations of the business that was funded.

Each crowdfunding site has differing requirements and operating procedures that you will want to understand before moving forward. For example, Kickstarter requires that the funding project achieve 100 percent of its funding goal or the project is not funded. In other words, the business will not receive any of the committed dollars if you do not reach 100 percent of the stated financing goal.

IndieGoGo does not hold to the 100 percent funding requirement that Kickstarter does, but you will, however, be charged a larger fee if you do not reach your stated goal. These sites generally charge a percentage of the total amount raised.

Below are 11 tips to raise money from people you do not know, which come from Rick Brooks, who wrote an informative article on crowdfunding on the *Social-Media Examiner* blog.[72]

1. Choose the right crowdfunding site for your business or project.

2. Know your target market.

3. Plan ahead.

4. Passionately pitch your project.

5. Have a plan for spending their money.

6. Leverage your social networks.

7. Break up bigger projects.

8. Create compelling rewards.

9. Treat our crowdfunding like a campaign.

10. Tell a great story and ask for the sale.

11. Promise and give credit where credit is due.

**Vendor Financing/Client Financing** is financing that may be available from one or more of your vendors, suppliers, or clients. Generally, this type of financing is available if one of your vendors or clients is a sizable company with a long history of working well with your company and wants you to expand to support their own expansion.

For example, if you want financing in order to expand your operations, and such expansion will allow you to purchase significantly more product from one of your major vendors, that vendor may be willing to provide financing to you (and potentially on favorable terms). Additionally, if a client loves your products or services and wants to purchase more from your company, you may be able to win financing from that client in order to support them.

Be careful in moving forward with this type of financing. If you pursue this path, your vendor or client will request significant financial detail of your business, which may come back to haunt you, if they believe you are making too much money and they want to renegotiate your contracts. However, your major vendors and clients are the ones who know you best and may be willing to back your business.

**Factoring** is selling a company's receivables to a third party to obtain funding. This is a $150 billion a year industry and is a common method of freeing up money your firm has tied up in working capital.[73] While factoring can create additional cash for your business, it is a short-term loan, not long-term financing.

To interest a lender that does factoring, your company must have consistent and significant accounts receivables, so this is not for a startup. A lender that does factoring is less interested in your creditworthiness and is more focused on the payment history of your customers, since they will be receiving the dollars collected from your clients paying their bills.

Your company's creditworthiness is also going to be analyzed, however, since certain clients may not pay their bills if they believe your company may be going bankrupt. Factoring can be an expensive method of getting short-term capital, but it can be helpful for some established businesses. Do your research and select a reputable company if you intend to take this route.

**Government grants and contracts** may be a possibility for your company, but understand it can be a lengthy process. Government grants are administered by specific agencies and for specific purposes. These grants are provided to companies to further specific public policy objectives, and can vary widely based on the specific agency or specific policy objective.

One of the biggest issues is to find the specific grant opportunity that may be appropriate for you and your company. Go to www.grants.gov or to the Catalogue of Federal Domestic Assistance (www.cfda.gov) to get more information on the opportunities currently available.

There are special programs for technology grants the SBA offers: the Small Business Innovation Research (SBIR) program and the Small Business Technology Transfer (STTR) program. These programs offer grants to technology companies that conduct specific research and development projects that are likely to have commercial applications. For more information, go to http://www.sba.gov/content/small-business-technology-trans fer-program-sttr and www.SBIR.gov. As noted previously, you can go to the local SBA office and speak to a counselor.

On the topic of potential government opportunities, while contracts are not financing, they can be helpful to building your business. If you want to learn more about winning government contracts for your company, there is a program called Business Matchmaking (www.Busi nessMatchmaking.com). This program matches corporate and government procurement buyers with small businesses. Since large corporations and government agencies have an incentive to advertise their work with small businesses, they seek small businesses to partner with on many projects.

Do not overlook state, county and city programs in your area. They are usually handled through an economic development agency (though it can have a variety of names) and focus on growing the local economy. A good place to start is to review the Economic Development Directory at www.ecdevdirectory.com. In addition, do not overlook the U.S. Small Business Administration (www.sba.gov), which offers many instructional courses to help you maneuver this process.

## Summary

I wrote this book to help entrepreneurs win the financing they need to grow their business. As the major job creators of the American economy, we need to ensure that small businesses get all the help they need to get themselves and the country on a prosperous path.

By implementing the strategies and using the information provided, your chances of winning financing should increase substantially. Do not get overwhelmed if you feel that you are not ready to move on financing today. You now have the roadmap to understand what you need to do to make sure that you are prepared to approach lenders or investors.

There are many sources you can approach to get help in taking the next steps and I have mentioned them throughout the book. Also, please go to our website, the Weklar Business Institute (www.WeklarBusinessInsti tute.com), for additional information, resources and training programs. If you desire more intensive training or support, see our coaching programs.

Also, while you are on the Weklar Business Institute site, sign up for our blog, *Winning Business Financing*, at www.WeklarBusinessInstitue.com/blog to learn about innovative strategies and best practices to grow your business and obtain financing for your company.

# Appendix A

# Consumer and Business Market Segmentation

The goal of customer segmentation is to assemble potential buyers into meaningful segments. Ask: "Is this segment worth pursuing and profitable?

Consumer and business segments are carved out in different ways. To help you develop effective marketing segments, use the consumer and business segmentation lists below and on the next page. This process should help you to identify your ideal or target markets.

## Consumer Segmentation

Consumer Segmentation is grouped into four categories: 1) geographic, 2) demographic, 3) psychographic or 4) behavioral. The table[74] below shows this segmentation.

| Segment | Segment Variables | Typical Breakdowns |
|---------|-------------------|---------------------|
| Geographic | City | Under 10,000; 10,000-24,999; etc |
| | Region | Northeast, South, West, etc |
| | Statistical Area | Metropolitan Statistical Area (MSA), Census Tract, etc. |
| | Media-Television | 210 designated market areas (DMA), Nielson |
| | Density | Urban; suburban, rural, etc. |

| Segment | Segment Variables | Typical Breakdowns |
|---|---|---|
| Demographic | Age | Under 6, 6-11, 12-17, etc. |
| | Birth Era | Baby boomers, Gen X, etc |
| | Education | Some high school, GED, high school graduate, college, etc. |
| | Gender | Male, female |
| | Household Size | 1; 2; 3-4; 5 or more |
| | Income | Under $15,000; $15,000-24,999; etc. |
| | Life Stage | Infant, preschool, child, youth, etc. |
| | Marital Status | Single, married, separated, divorced, widowed, domestic partner |
| | Occupation | Managerial, profession, technical, sales, etc. |
| | Race/Ethnicity | African American, Asian, Hispanic, White/Caucasian, etc. |
| Psychographic | Lifestyle (Claritas PRIZM) | Blue blood estates, single city blues, (66 neighborhood clusters in this approach) |
| | Needs | Quality, service, price/value, health, convenience, etc. |
| | Personality | Ambitious, aggressive, extroverted, introverted, etc. |
| | Values (VALS2) | Achievers, believers, innovators, thinkers, etc |
| Behavioral | Awareness/Intentions | Unaware, aware, interested, intending to buy, etc. |
| | Direct Marketing | Internet, catalog, door-to-door, direct response, etc. |
| | Product Features | Situation specific, general |
| | Retail Store Type | Department, outlet, specialty, convenience, etc. |
| | Usage Rates | Light user, medium user, heavy user |
| | User Status | Nonuser, ex-user, prospect, first-time user, regular user |

## Business Market Segmentation

The Business market can be segmented in three broad groupings as shown in the table[75] below:

1) geographic

2) demographic

3) behavioral

| Segment | Segment Variables | Typical Breakdowns |
|---------|-------------------|--------------------|
| Geographic | Statistical Areas | Metropolitan Statistical Area (MSA), Census Tract |
| | Density | Urban, suburban, small town, rural, etc. |
| | Country or Global Region | US, Japan, European Union, Asia, etc. |
| Demographic | Annual Sales | Under $1 million; $1 million-$9.9 million; etc. |
| | Number of Employees | 1-50; 51-99; 100-499, etc. |
| | NAICS Code | 2 digit: sector; 3 digit: subsector; 4 digit: industry; etc. |
| | NAICS Sector | Agriculture, forestry (11); mining (21); etc. |
| Behavioral | Application | Office, production, etc. |
| | Kind | Product, service |
| | Number of Locations | 1-9; 10-49; 50-99; etc. |
| | Purchase Location | Centralized, decentralized |
| | Type of Buy | New buy, modified rebuy, straight rebuy |
| | Where Used | Installation, component, supplies, etc. |
| | Who Buys | Individual buyer, industrial buying group, etc. |

An interesting example which shows both business and consumer segmentation is Apple® with its computers which are products that can be sold to both segments. Apple® targets its various lines of Mac® computers at specific market segments. The table[76] below suggests the market segmentation that Apple® used in developing their marketing plans for the products they had in 2011.

| Markets | | Computer Products | | | | |
|---|---|---|---|---|---|---|
| Sector | Segment | Mac Pro | MacBook Pro | iMac | MacBook Air | Mac Mini |
| Consumer | Individuals | ✓ | ✓ | ✓ | ✓ | ✓ |
| | Small/Home Office | | ✓ | ✓ | ✓ | |
| | Students | | | ✓ | ✓ | ✓ |
| | Teachers | | ✓ | ✓ | | |
| Professional | Medium/Small Business | ✓ | ✓ | ✓ | ✓ | |
| | Creative | ✓ | ✓ | ✓ | | |
| | College Faculty | | ✓ | ✓ | ✓ | |
| | College Staff | | | ✓ | | ✓ |

## Getting Started

The first step in this process is to identify the market segments that already exist in your client base. You can then create service offerings that really hit the mark. On the next page is a table that provides an example of the first step in client segmentation.

First divide your clients by market or industry group and identify the products and services you are providing to each client. The table on the next page represents an example for a strategic marketing consulting firm.

| Client/Customer | Market Segment | Product/Service Purchased |
|---|---|---|
| Client A | Technology | Strategic Planning |
| Client B | Individual | Career Counseling |
| Client C | Professional Services | Branding, Marketing Strategy |
| Client D | Retail | Promotional Programs |

Once you have completed identifying the segments for all your customers, use the worksheet below to create a list for each segment (e.g., manufacturing, professional services, technology, etc.).

## Market Specific Client Segmentation Worksheet

SEGMENT_____

| Client | Annual Revenues | | | | | Products & Services | |
|---|---|---|---|---|---|---|---|
| | Year 1 | Year 2 | Year 3 | Year 4 | Year 5 | Type | Revenue |
| | | | | | | | |
| | | | | | | | |
| | | | | | | | |
| | | | | | | | |
| | | | | | | | |
| | | | | | | | |
| | | | | | | | |

Conducting a segmentation analysis and creating market-specific client segmentation lists will give you:

- Segments you represent.

- Products/services you provide to each segment.

- Revenue generated for each segment.

This will provide you with the information needed to understand how to grow customers in each segment, and what additional products and/or services can be provided to expand that market segment. Chapter 6, *Marketing Strategies and Execution*, provides more detailed information regarding how to use research to identify your target market and ideal customers.

Your marketing strategies should be based in large part on your client segmentation, as well as research on the trends in the industries you represent. This will enable you to establish effective marketing strategies to reach your goals.

# Appendix B

# Financial Ratios

Financial professionals have their own language. In many cases, they speak in ratios. While you don't have to become totally proficient, you need to understand the financial basics to converse effectively with funding sources.

Ratios are the financial short-hand that funding sources use to show trends and variations that can help manage the business. There are several usual and customary ratios that you should present as part of your presentation to your financial source. Below we will show you the formula used to determine each ratio.

## Profitability Ratios

A Profit Margin will show how efficiently you are managing expenses:

$$\text{Profit Margin} = \frac{\text{Net Income}}{\text{Sales}}$$

Return on Assets lists how well assets are used to generate profit:

$$\text{Return on Assets} = \frac{\text{Net Profit}}{\text{Total Assets}}$$

Return on Investment (ROI) is the measure used to evaluate the efficiency of an investment or to compare the efficiency of a number of different investments.

$$\text{ROI} = \frac{\text{Gain from Investment} - \text{Cost of Investment}}{\text{Cost of Investment}}$$

This ratio can also measure either revenue or assets:

$$\text{Return on Sales} = \frac{\text{Net Profit}}{\text{Net Sales}}$$

$$\text{Return on Investment} = \frac{\text{Net Profit}}{\text{Average total Assets}}$$

## Liquidity or Solvency Ratios

Current Ratio shows if you can pay short-term debts:

$$\text{Current Ratio} = \frac{\text{Current Assets}}{\text{Current Liabilities}}$$

Total Debt Ratio describes the amount of leverage you have:

$$\text{Total Debt Ratio} = \frac{\text{Total Debt}}{\text{Total Assets}}$$

## Debt Management and Asset Ratios

Times Interest Earned can identify if there is enough income to pay the interest on debt:

$$\text{Times Interest Earned} = \frac{\text{EBIT*}}{\text{Accounts Payable}}$$

*Earnings Before Interest and Taxes*

Inventory Turnover details how long it takes to sell products:

$$\text{Inventory Turnover} = \frac{\text{COGS*}}{\text{Inventory}}$$

*Cost of Goods Sold*

Payables Turnover determines how quickly a company pays its suppliers:

$$\text{Payables Turnover} = \frac{\text{COGS}}{\text{Accounts Payable}}$$

Account Receivables Turnover identifies the length of time before a company receives payment for goods sold:

$$\text{Account Receivable Turnover} = \frac{\text{Sales}}{\text{Accounts Receivable}}$$

$$\text{Accounts Receivable Turnover} = \frac{\text{Credit Sales}}{\text{Average Receivable Balance}}$$

To give you an example of how these ratios are developed, here's how you would determine an Accounts Receivable Turnover. Let's say that ABC Company's annual credit sales were $400,000. At the beginning of the year, the accounts receivable balance was $55,000. The year-end balance was $45,000. The turn-over rate was calculated to be eight (8) times.

To determine your company's turnover rate, follow the steps below:

1. The average receivable balance for the company is $50,000 ($55,000 + $45,000 divided by 2).

2. The company's turnover ratio is $400,000 divided by $50,000.

   This indicates that receivables were converted over into cash 8 times during the year.

3. Number of Days in Receivables = 365 Days in the Year divided by the Turnover Ratio.

   Using the same information from the previous example gives us 46 days on average to collect our accounts receivable for the year.

## EBITDA

Some investors may ask for your company's historical and projected EBITDA. The term EBITDA is an acronym for earnings before interest, taxes, depreciation and amortization.

To determine EBITDA, all interest payments, tax, depreciation and amortization entries in the income statement are removed from the bottom-line net income. It is intended to measure and enable profitability comparison between different companies by:

- Canceling the effects of different asset bases by cancelling depreciation.

- Comparing different takeover histories by cancelling amortization often stemming from such items as goodwill.

- Evaluating the effects due to different tax structures, as well as the effects of different capital structures by cancelling interest payments on loans, mortgages, leases, etc.

The EBITDA of a company gives an indication on the operational profitability of the business. In other words, It points out how much profit the company makes with its present assets and its operations on the products it produces and sells. This takes into account possible provisions that need to be carried out.

A negative EBITDA indicates that a business may be investing for growth or has fundamental problems with its cost structure. A positive EBITDA, on the other hand, does not necessarily mean that the business generates cash. This is because EBITDA ignores changes in such things as working capital (usually needed when growing a business), capital expenditures (needed to replace assets that have broken down), taxes, and interest.

Your CPA will help you determine which ratios are appropriate for your business.

## Sales & Marketing Metrics

Marketing metrics enable you to demonstrate the contribution that marketing and sales strategies make to the company's bottom line and to the efficiency of these investments—the marketing ROI. Below are some important metrics that the business needs to determine how well their marketing investment is paying off.

### *Customer Retention*

$$\text{Customer retention} = \frac{\text{Customers Retained}}{\text{Total Customers at start of year} \times 100\%}$$

Let's show you an example of how this formula is used:

$$67\% = \frac{67}{100 \times 100\%}$$

This formula tells us that this business retains 67 percent of its customer base each year. This means this business must obtain 33 new customers each year just to maintain its base of 100 customers.

You must remember to add in the cost of customer acquisition—which typically is 7 to 10 times (or even more) the cost of maintaining a customer. This is a huge opportunity cost that is lost and could have been more effectively spent expanding your client base.

So if you can increase retention rates, you will save a significant sum of money and improve profitability. Also, as previously stated, a returning customer tends to spend more money with you than a new one. In addition, by showing lenders and investors how well you have improved customer retention, you will demonstrate to them how well you are employing efficient sales and marketing strategies. If asking for funding to bring on sales and marketing staff to focus on retention issues, you can use these numbers in your forecasting.

## Net Marketing Contribution

Marketing profitability is based on marketing and sales investments that the company made to achieve specific goals. The net marketing contribution can be used as a metric of marketing profitability.

Net Marketing Contribution (NMC) =

1. Sales Revenue x % of Gross Revenue = $x

2. $x minus Marketing & Sales Expenses = NMC

Using Apple's 2009 financial data (see table below), their net marketing contribution was $10 Billion:

$10 Billion = $36.54 billion X 36% - $3.12 billion

| APPLE 2009 | |
|---|---|
| **Performance** | **Apple, Inc** |
| Sales | $36.54B |
| Percent Gross Profit | 36% |
| Gross Profit | $13.15B |
| Marketing and Sales Expenses (%) | 8.6% |
| Marketing and Sales Expenses | $3.12B |
| **Net Marketing Contribution** | **$10.03B** |
| General & Administrative Expenses (%) | 2.8% |
| Other Expenses (% Sales) | 3.6% |
| Operating Income | $7.66B |
| Interest & Taxes (%Operating Income) | 25.6% |
| **Net Profit After Tax** | **$5.70B** |
| Earnings Per Share | $6.29 |

## Marketing Returns

Financial sources want to know how much of a return you make on your investments. The ROI regarding your marketing investment is no exception. The formulas to determine your marketing and sales ROI is below:

$$\text{Marketing ROI} = \frac{\text{Net Marketing Contribution}}{\text{Marketing \& Sales Expenses}}$$

$$\text{Marketing ROS*} = \frac{\text{Net Marketing Contribution}}{\text{Sales}}$$

*Return on Sales

Once you have these metrics you can benchmark against companies within your industry. You can look at public companies in your industry, or you can talk with a trade association that represents your industry to obtain this information.

# Appendix C

# Creating Business Credit Profiles

### Dun and Bradstreet (D&B)

D&B is one of the easiest ways to open a business credit profile.

- Start with Getting a D-U-N-S Number.

  - Free D-U-N-S number

    - Takes about 60 days after you have completed the form process.

      You will be given options to purchase expedited process to get a D-U-N-S number.

**NOTE:** *Having your D&B number faster does NOT speed up the entire process of building business credit.*

  - D&B Credit Profile

    - You can create a D&B credit profile as a package service where you get a number and profile created the same day if you pay for the service.

- With Free Service, You Still Get the Same Outcome

  - You will be told that if you don't pay for D&B profile service, your account is not activated.

    - This is correct; however, once you have a vendor or creditor report activity on your company, your profile is created and account is immediately activated.

  - Once you have your free D-U-N-S number:

    - Please remember that you can pull your own report. Once a vendor or creditor reports your payment history, your profile is created and activated immediately.

  - To confirm if your account is activated:

    - You can find your company after performing a D&B search by purchasing a company profile report.

      If your company currently does not have a D&B profile, a report will not be created for you; therefore, your credit card will not be charged for a report.

      If you confirmed that your profile is active, you can purchase a copy of your D&B report.

  - D&B support is composed of commission sales people.

    - You can create your corporate credit profile and build business credit without buying expensive programs.

- D&B Credit Score

  – D&B uses a multi-tiered approach to rating businesses call "Paydex" along with D-U-N-S system (Data Universal Numbering System).

  – Paydex uses a 20 to 100 numerical score.

    • 80 to 100 are good scores

      80 = prompt payment

    • 70 and below are poor

      70 = slow 15
      50 = slow 30
      40 = slow 60

  – D&B also uses a simple 1 to 4 credit rating system.

    • 1 = high
    • 2 = good
    • 3 = fair
    • 4 = limited

## Experian Credit Profile

Like the reports from the other business credit-reporting agencies, Experian's credit profile shows activity from many sources, including revolving credit providers, banks and other financing institutions, equipment leasing companies, suppliers, and more.

- Perform a company search with Experian to see if your company already has a profile created.

- Search by company name (without Inc., Corp, LLC) and provide your location details.

- Finding your firm means an active profile.

- You can purchase a credit report on any company found on Experian. The cost depends on the report you select.

- If No Profile and Cannot Pull Reports

  - Don't worry; once you have open lines of credit reporting to Experian your file will grow.

- Credit Scoring

  - There are two systems: Intelliscore and the Vantage score.

    - Intelliscore

      ✓ Designed to predict payment delinquencies in excess of 90 days.

      ✓ Assigns risk score from 0 to 100.

      ✓ Higher scores denote less risk.

    - Vantage

      ✓ Intended to level different scoring systems of various rating agencies.

      ✓ Differing scores from other agencies are result of different parameters and not merely different scores for the same credit issues.

✓ Scores are aligned consistently across different credit reporting companies to create a scale from 501-990.

✓ Correspond to simple A, B, C, D, and F.

901-990 = A
801-900 = B
701-800 = C
601-700 = D
501-600 = F

## Equifax Credit Profile

Once your business has a line of credit from a bank or bank issues credit cards you will be listed with Equifax.

- An Equifax corporate credit file is not available at any time like D&B or Experian.

    – Can be obtained when you need it.

        • When a lender requests a report

            ✓ Equifax only give reports to lenders that you authorize so will know who is receiving your information.

        • Giving authorization to an organization

            ✓ Request your own copy from Equifax.

        • If credit was denied based on an Equifax report

            ✓ If you have been denied, you have 60 days to contact Equifax.

- Credit scoring

  - Predicts delinquency on financial accounts and is designed for the financial services industry.

  - Numeric—between 101-992 with lower score denoting a greater risk of delinquency.

  - Delivers four "reason Codes" that serve to indicate which factors more greatly affected the score.

  - Uses a "Commercial Score" system that separates "trade" credit from other credit (leases, etc.).

    - Assumption is that businesses are more likely to meet real estate, lease or banking lines of credit obligations over trade-related obligations.

    - These scores attempt to predict the type of accounts most likely to be defaulted upon.

# About the Author

Diane Weklar, often referred to as the "authority on accelerating business growth," is an innovative business strategist, exciting speaker and powerful author. She has been igniting business profits for 25 years in the corporate and consulting arenas. She is also a serial entrepreneur.

With this unique combination of industry knowledge, her forte is synchronizing strategic goals with business operations to achieve peak performance. She is adept at identifying and pursuing aggressive growth opportunities in both strong and weak economic markets.

In addition to consulting to a broad base of companies, Diane is a serial entrepreneur who has launched a number of ventures that provide eCommerce solutions to government entities, a web-based recruitment portal, and an energy advocacy group. She also co-founded the first company to provide corporate marketing and management tools to the legal industry.

Currently the CEO of the Weklar Business Institute, Diane provides training and coaching on a variety of services to small and medium-sized businesses, including strategic execution, integrated marketing solutions, performance optimization, and obtaining capital. In addition, she is President of the Weklar Consulting Group, an international consulting firm.

An adjunct professor at the University of Redlands and sought-after advisor, she has presented at and written extensively for many organizations. A true trainer, she uses real-life examples and cutting-edge research to provide innovative, step-by-step methods for success through her presentations, training, and books.

Diane has an MBA in Finance and Marketing and a B.A. in Economics.

If you would like Diane to help your firm grow, have her speak to your group, or if you wish to sign up for her blog, *Winning Business Financing,* please visit her website, www.WeklarBusinessInstitute.com.

# Invite Diane Weklar to Speak at Your Event

## Contact Diane Today!

Call:  951.263.9089
eMail: Diane@Weklar.com

## SCHEDULE Diane for your next conference:

- ➤ Keynotes
- ➤ Breakout Sessions
- ➤ Training Programs
- ➤ Retreats
- ➤ Association Meetings

**Diane Weklar** is the Authority on Accelerating Business Growth!  An exciting and powerful innovator, author, and strategist, helping you build a successful business in any economy!

A gifted speaker, Diane Weklar has taught countless business professionals how to accelerate growth and profits. She has been igniting business growth and profits for 25 years in the corporate and consulting arenas, as well as a serial entrepreneur. Diane is the author of ***Mastering the Money Maze: 10 Secrets to Winning Business Financing***, which provides practical insight for business owners and managers who need to raise capital.

Presentation topics are customized for your audience and can include:

- ➤ **The 10 Secrets to Winning Business Financing**
- ➤ **Secrets that High Performance Companies Use to Beat the Competition!**
- ➤ **I Market, So Why Am I Not Growing**
- ➤ **Ignite the Opportunities Hiding in Your Customer Base**

## For more information go to:

www.WeklarBusinessInstitute.com/business-speakers

# WINNING BUSINESS FINANCING BOOTCAMP
## *A Hands-On, Interactive Workshop*

### *For Business Leaders Who Want Lenders and Investors to say YES! You're Approved*

Join Diane Weklar as she hosts *Mastering the Money Maze: 10 Secrets to Winning Business Financing.* This program will provide you with practical training, customized to your personal needs, to help you win the financing you need to grow your business. This program provides step-by-step coaching for all the aspects to help you create a winning proposal including:

✓ Identify the best financing sources for your business

✓ Demystify the process of successfully working with funders

✓ Develop a persuasive presentation to lenders and investors

✓ Develop successful business plans and business models

✓ Present the attractiveness of investing in your business

✓ Articulate your growth strategies effectively

✓ And much, much more

Diane Weklar has been igniting business growth for over 20 years. She is the CEO of the Weklar Business Institute providing training and coaching in strategic execution, integrated marketing and performance optimization. She is the author *of Mastering the Money Maze: 10 Secrets of Winning Business Financing,* to help small and mid-sized businesses obtain the capital they need to grow.

### *For more information go to* **www.WeklarBusinessInstitute.com**

292

# WEKLAR
# BUSINESS INSTITUTE

The Weklar Business Institute is the brainpower hub for accelerating your business growth. We provide online and onsite training and coaching in a variety of areas including:

- ➢ Strategic Execution
- ➢ Integrated Marketing
- ➢ Performance Optimization
- ➢ Winning Financing

Our mission is to provide business owners and managers with all the strategies, tools and processes they need to accelerate their growth. We believe in helping entrepreneurs achieve what they really want—a thriving business that runs like a well-oiled machine and produces substantial profits.

Our Blog **Winning Business Financing** provides tips, techniques, and cutting-edge research to help small and mid-sized businesses obtain the lender and investor financing they need to grow their businesses.

*SIGN UP TO OUR FREE BLOG AND GET A SPECIAL BONUS AT:*
www.WeklarBusinessInstitute.com/blog

*REGISTER FOR OUR UPCOMING TRAINING PROGRAMS AT:*
www.WeklarBusinessInstitute.com/events

REVIEW OUR ONGOING PROGRAMS AT:
www.WeklarBusinessInstitute.com/programs

WANT DIANE WEKLAR TO SPEAK AT YOUR EVENT? Get more information at:
www.WeklarBusinessInstitute.com/business-speakers

# Further Reading

## *Business Plans/Models*

Benton, Angela, "Don't Get Stuck in the Minutia," The Wall Street Journal/The Accelerators, 27 November, 2012, < http://blogs.wsj.com/accelerators/2012/11/27/hook-investors-with-a-concise-plan/>

Blank, Steve, "Part I: Validate Your Business Model Start with a Business Model, Not a Business Plan," The Wall Street Journal/The Accelerators, 26 November, 2012, <http://blogs. wsj.com/accelerators/2012/11/26/start-with-a-business-model-not-a-business-plan/>

Blank, Steve, "Part I: Validate Your Business Model," The Wall Street Journal /The Accelerators, 29 November, 2012, <http://blogs.wsj.com/accelerators/2012/11/29/validate-your-business-model/>

Hauk, Helena, "What Lenders Look for in a Business Plan," BPlans, Up and Running Blog, 2 May, 2011, <http://upandrunning.bplans.com/2011/05/02/what-lenders-look-for-in-a-business-plan/>

Hirschfield, Alexa, "Distill Your Ideas Into an Overview," The Wall Street Journal/The Accelerators, 28 November, 2012, http://blogs.wsj.com/accelerators/2012/11/28/distill- your-ideas-into-an-overview/

Lee, Paul, "Your Business Plan Isn't a Fundraising Tool Anymore," The Wall Street Journal/The Accelerators, 28 November, 2012, http://blogs.wsj.com/accelerators/2012/11/28/your-business-plan-isnt-a-fundraising-tool-anymore/>

Master, Marc, "Business plans and their importance and 78% of businesses do not have one," Examiner.com, 22May, 2010, <http://www.examiner.com/article/business-plans-and-their importance-and-78%-of-businesses-do-not-have-one>

Osterwalder, Alexander, "Burn Your Business Plan – Before it Burns You," The Wall Street Journal/The Accelerators, 26 November, 2012, http://blogs.wsj.com/accelerators/2012/11/12/burn-your-business-plan-before-it-burns-you/>

Ravikant, Naval, "First See If People Want What You Are Building," The Wall Street Journal/The Accelerators, 28 November, 2012, <http://blogs.wsj.com/accelerators/2012/11/28/first-see-if-people-want-what-youre-building/>

Tisch, David, "Do a Ton of Homework Before Writing a Business Plan," The Wall Street Journal/The Accelerators, 26 November, 2012, http://blogs.wsj.com/accelerators/2012/11/26/do-a-ton-of-homework-before-writing-a-business-plan/

Zimmerman, Ed, "Part I: The Impending Series A Funding Cliff and You! The Wall Street Journal/The Accelerators, 26 November, 2012, <http://blogs.wsj.com/accelerators/2012/11/26/the-impending-series-a-funding-cliff-and-you/>

Zimmerman, Ed, "Part II: It's Not What's In the Plan — It's What You Do With It! The Wall Street Journal/The Accelerators, 29 November, 2012, <http://blogs.wsj.com/accelerators/2012/11/29/its-not-whats-in-the-plan-its-what-you-do-with-it/>

### Credit

"Biz2Credit Analysis of Women-Owned Businesses Identifies Challenges for Female Entrepreneurs Seeking Small Business Loans," PRWire, 27 March, 2013, <http://www.prweb.com/releases/women/smallbusiness/prweb10573154.htm>

"Corporate Credit and Your Company Financial Position," Companies Incorporated, <http://www.companiesinc.com/services/corporate-credit/build-credit-yourself8.asp>

"Corporate Credit FAQ," Companies Incorporated, <http://www.companiesinc.com/services/corporate-credit/faq.asp>

"Corporate Credit with a Dun and Bradstreet Profile," Companies Incorporated, <http://www.companiesinc.com/services/corporate-credit/build-credit-yourself4.asp>

"Corporate Credit Score," Companies Incorporated,< http://www.companiesinc.com/services/corporate-credit/scores. asp

Hendricks, Evan, Credit Scores & Credit Reports: How the System Really Works, What You Can Do (Evan Hendricks and Privacy Times, Inc., 2004),

"How to Get a Business Credit Card with Bad Credit," Card Hub <http://www.cardhub.com/edu/business-credit-card-with-no-personal-guarantee/>

Loten, Angus, "Credit Reports: What Small Businesses Don't Know Can Hurt Them," Wall Street Journal, 13 June, 2013,<http://online.wsj.com/article/ SB10001424127887323893504578559420352637566.html?mod=small_business_newsreel>

"Managing Credit – Made Simpler," Council of Better Business Bureaus, http://www.bbb.org/credit-management/ Managing-Credit-Made-Simpler_Small-Businesses .pdf

Markowtiz, Eric, "How to Build and Maintain Good Business Credit," INC., 30 November, 2010, <http://www.inc.com/guides/2010/11/how-to-build-and-maintain-good-business-credit.html>

Roussell, Norman David, Principles of Building Business Credit (Start Smart, 2007)

Sandler, Dan, "The New World of Business Credit," All Business, <http://www.allbusiness.com/banking-finance/banking-finance-overview/15608024-1.html>

Todorova, Aleksandra, "Five Things to Know About Small Business Plastic," Smart Money, 7 July, 2007, < http://www.smartmoney.com/spend/family-money/five-things-to-know-about-small-business-plastic-14925/>

### Debt vs. Equity

Advani, Asheesh, "Choosing Between Debt and Equity Financing," Entrepreneur, 3 April, 2006, <http://www.entrepreneur.com/article/159518#>

"Choosing Between Debt and Equity Financing,"<http://www.go4funding.com/Articles/Business-Funding/Choosing-Between-Debt-and-Equity-Financ ing.aspx>

"Debt vs. Equity – Advantages and Disadvantages," Findlaw Small Business, <http://smallbusiness. findlaw.com/busin ess-finances/debt-vs-equity-advantages-and-disadvantages. html>

"Debt vs. Equity Financing: Which Is the Best Way for Your Business to Access Capital?" National Federation of Indepen dent Business, < http://www.nfib.com/business-resources/business-resources-item?cmsid=50036>

"Differences Between Angel Investors and Venture Capitalists," <http://www.go4funding.com/Articles/Business-Funding/Differences-Between-Angel-Investors-And-Venture-Capitalists.aspx>

### Entrepreneurs

Conner, Cheryl, "Who's Starting America's New Businesses? And Why?" Forbes, 22 July, 2012, <http://www.forbes.com/sites/cherylsnappconner/2012/07/22/whos-starting-americas-new-businesses-and-why/>

Huhman, Heather, "9 Questions to Ask Yourself when Considering Entrepreneurship," Careerealism, <http://www.careerealism.com/questions-entrepreneurship/>

Farlie, Robert W., Kauffman Index of Entrepreneurial Activity, Ewing Marion Kauffman Foundation, 2012 <http://www.kaufmann.org>

Farrell, Chris, "Older Entrepreneurs Start Companies Too," Bloomberg Businessweek, 30 April, 2012, <http://www.businessweek.com/articles/2012-04-30/older-entrepreneurs-start-companies-too>

"Frequently Asked Questions about Small Business," U.S. Small Business Administration, September, 2012

"Kauffman FastFacts: Entrepreneurship and the Economy," Ewing Marian Kauffman Foundation, November, 2011 <http://www.kauffman.org/uploaded files/factsheet/entrep_and_economy_fast_facts.pdf>

Kelley, Donna J., Ali, Abdul, Rogoff, Edward G, et al, National Entrepreneurial Assessment for the United States of America 2011, Global Entrepreneurship Monitor, 2011

Klein, Karen E., "Why Entrepreneurship Is Declining, Bloom berg Businessweek, 21 March, 2012, <http://www. business week.com/articles/2012-03-21/why-entrepre neurship-is-declining>

Klein, Karen E., "Startup Rates Surge in the U.S. and Abroad," Bloomberg Businessweek, 19 January, 2012 <http://www.businessweek.com/small-business/startup-rates-surge-in-the-us-and-abroad-01202012.html>

Maltby, Emily, "More Owners Help Finance Sales of Their Firms," The Wall Street Journal, 8 March, 2012

"National Women's Business Council 2012 Annual Report," National Women's Business Council, 2012, http://www.nwbc. gov/sites/default/files/NWBC_2012AnnualReport_FINAL.pdf>

O'Brien, Matthew, "The Terrifying Reality of Long-Term Unemployment," The Atlantic, 16 April, 2013, <http://www. theatlantic.com/business/archive/2013/04/the-terrifying-reality-of-long-term-unemployment/ 274957/>

Rampell, Catherine, "In Hard Economy for All Ages, Older Isn't Better...It's Brutal," New York Times, 2 February, 2013 <http://www.nytimes.com/2013/02/03/business/americans-closest-to-retirement-were-hardest-hit-by-recession. html?pa gewanted=all&_r=0>

Shah, Dharmesh, "12 Facts About Entrepreneurs That Will Likely Surprise You," OnStartups, 21 September, 2009, <http://onstartups.com/tabid/3339/bid/10561/ 12-Facts-About-Entrepreneurs-That-Will-Likely-Surprise-You.aspx>

Shontell Alyson, "10 Questions About Why Some Entre preneurs Fail and Others Succeed," Business Insider, 8 December, 2010, <http://www.careerealism.com/questions-entrepreneurship/>

Sirkin, Harold C., "Unleashing American's Entrepreneurial Power," BloombergBusinessweek, 13 April, 2012, <http://www.businessweek.com/articles/2012-04-13/unleashing-america-s-entrepreneurial-power>

Stangler, Dane, "The Coming Entrepreneurship Boom," Ewing Marion Kauffman Foundation, June 2009.

Tausig, Alex, "15 Mistakes Young Entrepreneurs Make, But Don't Have To," Fortune, 4 January, 2011 <http://finance.forturne.cnn.com/2011/01/04/15-mistakes-young-entrepreneurs-make-but-dont-have-to/

McPeak, Isabella, "Family Business Statistics in the US," Peak Family Business.com, 25  October, 2011 <http://peakfamilybusiness.com/2011/10/25/family-business-statistics-in-the-us/>

"Quiz: Are You Tough Enough?" Small Business Bible, Success Magazine Online, <http://www.success.com/articles/581--entrepreneurship-quiz>

Van Brussel, Joe, "National Association of Women Business Owners (NAWBO) President Talks Women and Small Business," Huffington Post, 1 March, 2013 <http://www.huffingtonpost.com/2013/04/01/the-national-association-women-business-owners-nawbo_ n_2971335.html>

"Women-Owned Businesses in the 21st Century," U.S. Department of Commerce Economics and Statistics Administration for the White House Council on Women and Girls, October 2010

### *Financing*

Burk, James E., Lehmann, Richard P., Financing Your Small Business (Sourcebooks, Inc., 2006)

Fullen, Sharon, How to Get the Financing for Your New Small Business: Innovative Solutions from the Experts Who Do It Every Day (Atlantic Publishing Group, Inc., 2006).

Strauss, Steven D., Get Your Business Funded: Creative Methods for Getting the Money You Need (John Wiley & Sons, Inc., 2011),

***Investors***

Angel Capital Education Foundation <http://www. kauffman. org/entrepreneurship/angelcapitaleducationfoundation.aspx> "Angel Investor Statistics," Statistic Brain,  15 July, 2012 <http://www.statisticbrain.com/angel-investorstatistics/>

"By the Numbers," Private Equity Growth Capital Council, 2012 <http://www.pegcc.org/education/pe-by-the-num bers/>

"Dorsey & Whitney Survey Shows Robust Startup Funding Climate; Pendulum Swings Back to Institutional VCs, Who Make Strong Comeback," PRWeb, 26 April, 2013, <http://www.prweb.com/releases/Dorsey/CEO_Survey/prwe b9445221.htm>

Koetsier, John, "The rise of the angel investor (info graphic)," Venture Beat/Entrepreneur, 19 February, 2013, http://venturebeat.com/2013/02/19/the-rise-of-the-angel-investor-infographic/

Stark, Karl, Stewart, Bill, "Be Irresistible to Investors: 3 Steps," INC., 6 December, 2012 <http://www.inc.com/ karl-and-bill/be-irresistible-to-investors-3-steps.html>

Mulcahy, Diane, "Six Myths About Venture Capitalists," Harvard Business Review, May 2013 <http://hbr.org/ 2013/05/six-myths-about-venture-capitalists/ar/1>

National Venture Capital Association Yearbook 2012, National Venture Capital Association, 2012 (Thompson Reuters 2012)

"Private Equity," New York Times-Times Topics, 11 October, 2012

Sudek, Richard, May, Allan, Wiltbank, Robert, "Angel Investing: Catalyst for Innovation," October, 2011

### Lenders

Alliance Bank, "What Do Bankers Look for in a Business Loan Application" https://www.myalliancebank.com/ f8web/?uf=. /PDFs/What_Do_Bankers_look_for_in_a_Business(WebVersion).pdf

Clark, Patrick, "Why Women are Less Likely to Land Business Loans," Bloomberg Businessweek, 28 March, 2013, <http:// www.businessweek.com/articles/2013-03-28/why-women-are-less-likely-to-land-business-loans>

Lagorio, Christine, "9 Questions to Ask a Small Business Lender," Inc., 6 May, 2010 <http;//www.inc.com/guides/2010/05/9-discussions-to-have-with-your-banker-lender.html>

Quinn, Matt, "The Small-Business Lending Riddle," INC., 14 January, 2011 <http://www.inc.com/matt-quinn/ solving-the-small-business-lending-riddle.html>

Quinn, Matt, "Big Banks and Small Business," INC., 15 October, 2010, <http://www.inc.com/matt-quinn/big-banks-and-small-business.html>

Quinn, Matt, "What Loan Officers Want," INC. 11 October, 2010, <http://www.inc.com/matt-quinn/what-loan-offi cers-want.htm>

Rosenberg, Joseph L., "Presenting Small Business Financial Statements to a Lender: What you'll need to have in hand when you apply for a small business loan," About.com/Entre preneurs, <http://entrepreneurs.about .com/od/financing/a/finstatelender.htm >

Russakoff, Rich, Goodman, Mary, "10 Questions to Find the Right Bank for Your Business," CBS MoneyWatch, 6 April, 2011, <http://www.cbsnews.com/8301-505143_ 162-48640126/10-questions-to-find-the-right-bank-for-your-business/>

Ryan, Vincent, "When Banks Won't Touch Your Company: Alternative financing firms take on credit risks that financial institutions don't want," CFO.com, 10 October, 2012, <http://www3.cfo.com/article/2012/ 10/credit_ nonbank-capital-alternative-financing-risk-appetite-prudential-solar-basel-iii>

Senior, Glenn, targeting Small Business: How Banks can Drive Customer Loyalty and Growth with Business-focused Web Content, The Small Business Company, 2012

Wesson, Patricia H., Secrets Lenders Never Told You: How to Get Your Business Loan Approved! (Simple & Direct Publishing, 2005),

Wilson, Steven, "Commerical loans available for well-prepared businesses," Dayton Business Journal, 26 April, 2010 <http://www.bizjournals.com/dayton/stories/ 2010 /04/26/story6.html>

### *Marketing*

Aksu, Julya, "Customer Service: The New Proactive Marketing," Huff Post Business Blog, 26, March, 2013 <http://www.huffingtonpost.com/hulya-aksu/customer-service-the-new-_b_2827889.html>

Churchill, Neil C., Lewis, Virginia L., "Five Stages of Small Business Growth," Harvard Business Review, May-June, 1983

"Customer Service Facts," CSM-Customer Service Manager <http://www.customerservicemanager.com/ customer-service-facts.htm>

Ernst, Jeff, " Metrics That Matter for B2B Marketers: Revenue Impact Should Top the CMOs Management Dashboard," Forrester, 26 October, 2011, <http://www. smartb2bmarket ing.co.uk/uploads/3/0/7/8/3078654/forrester_metrics_that _matter_for_b2b_marketers_jeff_ernst_10.26.11.pdf>

Kerin, Roger A., Hartley, Steven W., Rudelius, William, Marketing (McGraw-Hill Irvwin, 2013)

"Know the Score: the Ultimate Guide to Scoring Custom ers and Prospects," Silverpop, 2013 <http://www. silver pop.com/downloads/white-papers/WP_Scoring2013.pdf>

Kruse, Kevin, "Zig Ziglar: 10 Quotes That Can Change Your Life," Forbes, 28 November, 2012 <http://www.forbes.com/ sites/kevinkruse/2012/11/28/zig-ziglar-10-quotes-that-can-change-your-life/>

Lawrence, Alex, "Five Customer Retention Tips for Entrepre-neurs," Forbes, 2 November, 2012 <http://www. forbes.com/ sites/alexlawrence/2012/11/01/five-customer-retention-tips-for-entrepreneurs/>

"Losing a Gorilla Client," Recourses, 3 January, 2013, <http://www.recourses.com/losing-gorilla-client>

Porter, Michael E., Competitive Strategy: Techniques for Analyzing Industries and Competitors, (Free Press, 1998)

Reichheld, Frederick, F., "The Economics of E Loyalty," Harvard Business School, 10 July, 2000 <http://hbswk.hbs.edu/archive/1590.html>

Rigby, Darrell, Lancry, Ouriel, "Winning in Turbulence: Price for Today and Tomorrow," Harvard Business Press, 2009, Bain & Company, Inc.

Shah, Darmesh, Inbound Marketing: Get Found Using Google, Social Media and Blogs, (John Wiley & Sons, Inc., 2009)

**Metrics / Dashboards**

Barry, Jeffrey, "Developing Your Corporate Dashboard of Key Performance Metrics," F. Curtis Barry & Company, <http://www.fcbco.com/articles-and-whitepapers/ articles/bid/129520/Developing-Your-Corporate-Dashboard-of-Key-Performance-Metrics>

Best, Roger J., "Getting Started Using Marketing Metrics: Whitepaper," Marketing Metrics Solutions, <http://www.marketingmetricssolutions.com/pdf/MMH%20-%20WP%20Final%20RB.pdf>

"Designing and Building Great Dashboards – 6 Golden Rules to Successful Dashboard Design," Geckoboard, 10 July, 2012 http://www.geckoboard.com/building-great-dashboards-6-golden-rules-to-successful-dashboard-design/

Spiro, Herbert T., Finance for the Non-Financial Manager: Fourth Edition (John Wiley & Sons, Inc., 1996).

Wise, Lyndsay W., "A Closer Look At Dashboards: The Essential Components Of Any Dashboard," Dashboard Insight, 20 April, 2010 <http://www.dashboardinsight.com/articles/digital-dashboards/fundamentals/a-closer-look-dashboards.aspxDashboard>

### *Personal Guarantees/Collateral*

Anthony, Joseph, "6 Things to Know About Getting an SBA Loan," Microsoft Business, 2011 <http://www .microsoft. com/business/en-us/resources/startups/ startup-financing/ 6-things-to-know-about-getting-an-sba-loan.aspx?fbid=KAd CMjPikRz>

Coughlin, James, "Personal Guarantees and Business Loans: A Primer for CPAs to Better Advise Their Clients," Accounting Today, 4 January, 2011 <http://www.accountingtoday.com/ news/Personal-Guarantees-Business-Loans-56798-1.html>

"How Can I Get A Business Credit Card With No Personal Guarantee?, Card Hub, http://www.cardhub.com/edu/ Business-Credit-Card-With-No-Personal-Guarantee/>

Lagoria, Christine, "What You Need to Know About Making a Personal Guarantee," INC>, 15 February, 2010 <http://www. inc.com/guides/personal-guarantee-making.html>

Markowitz, Eric, "5 Tips for Using Collateral to Secure a Small Business Loan," INC., 31 January, 2011<http://www.inc. com/guides/201101/5-tips-using-collateral-to-secure-a-small-business-loan.html>

SBA, "7(a) Loan Repayment Terms," U.S. Small Business Administration <http://www.sba.gov/content/7a-loan-repayment-terms

SBA, "Borrowing Money For Your Business," U.S. Small Business Administration <http://www.sba.gov content/ borrowing-money>

SBA, "Collateral" U.S. Small Business Administration,< http://www.sba.gov/content/collateral>

**Productivity/ Profitability**

Domingo, Rene T., "True Productivity: The Key to Profitability," RTDonline, 2003

Hayes, Mark, "Stop Obsessing Over Revenue: 3 Proven Strategies for Increasing Profitability," Shopify, 4 October, 2012, < http://www.shopify.com/blog/6657676-stop-obsessing-over-revenue-3-proven-strategies-for-increasing-profitability#axzz2XZ2vdShZ>

"Five Routes to Greater Profitability," PowerHomeBiz, 2013

*Proposals/Presentations*

Chautin, Jerry, "How to Make a Winning Loan Proposal: A Business Plan designed for getting a loan approved," The Entrepreneur Network, <http://tenonline.org/sref/jc1.html>

Gleason, Chris, "5 Steps to Presenting Deals to Private Lenders: Knowing how to package your loan request is key to securing funding," Scotsman Guide Commercial Edition, May, 2011, <http://www.scotsmanguide.com/default.asp?ID=4613&part=1>

Sandler, Dan, "Preparing a Financial Presentation for Lenders," AllBusiness.com, <http://www.allbusiness.com/banking-finance/banking-finance-overview/15608025-1.html>

*Statistics*

Angel Capital Education Foundation <http://www.kauffman.org/entrepreneurship/angelcapitaleducationfoundation.aspx>

"Angel Investor Statistics," Statistic Brain, 15 July, 2012 <http://www.statisticbrain.com/angel-investorstatistics/>

"Biz2Credit Analysis of Women-Owned Businesses Identifies Challenges for Female Entrepreneurs Seeking Small Business Loans," PRWire, 27 March, 2013, <<http://www.prweb.com/releases/women/smallbusiness/prweb10573154.htm<

"By the Numbers." Private Equity Growth Capital Council, 2012, http://www.pegcc.org/education/pe-by-the-numbers/

"Community Banking Facts," Independent Community Bankers of America, March, 2012 <http://www.icba.org/files/ICBASites/PDFs/cbfacts.pd>

"Dorsey & Whitney Survey Shows Robust Startup Funding Climate; Pendulum Swings Back to Institutional VCs, Who Make Strong Comeback," PRWeb, 26 April, 2013, http://www.prweb.com/releases/Dorsey/CEO_Survey/prweb9445221.htm

Dun & Bradstreet. (2011). The State of Small Businesses Post Great Recession: An Analysis of Small Businesses between 2007 and 2011. <htpp://www.dnbgov.com/pdf/DNB_SMB_Report_May2011.pdf>

Farlie, Robert W., Kauffman Index of Entrepreneurial Activity, Ewing Marion Kauffman Foundation, 2012,

Farrell, Chris, "Older Entrepreneurs Start Companies Too," Bloomberg Businessweek, 30 April, 2012, <http://www.businessweek.com/articles/2012-04-30/older-entrepreneurs-start-companies-too>

"Federal Deposit Insurance Corporation (FDIC) Number of Institutions, Branches and Total Offices, FDIC-Insured Commercial Banks US and other Areas," 2012 <http://www2.fdic.gov/hsob/HSOBRpt.asp>

"Frequently Asked Questions about Small Business," U.S. Small Business Administration, September, 2012

"Kauffman FastFacts: Entrepreneurship and the Economy," Ewing Marian Kauffman Foundation, November, 2011 <http://www.kauffman.org/uploadedfiles/factsheet/entrep_and_economy_fast_facts.pdf>

Kane, Tim, "The Importance of Startups in Job Creation and Job Destruction: Kauffman Foundation Research Series: Firm Formation and Economic Growth," Ewing Marion Dauffman Foundation, July, 2010

Kelley, Donna J., Ali, Abdul, Rogoff, Edward G, et al, National Entrepreneurial Assessment for the United States of America 2011, Global Entrepreneurship Monitor, 2011

Klein, Karen E., "Why Entrepreneurship Is Declining, Bloomberg Businessweek, 21 March, 2012, <http://www.businessweek.com/articles/2012-03-21/why-entrepreneurship-is-declining>

Maltby, Emily, "More Owners Help Finance Sales of Their Firms," The Wall Street Journal, 8 March, 2012

"National Women's Business Council 2012 Annual Report," National Women's Business Council, 2012, <http://www.nwbc.gov/sites/default/files/NWBC_2012AnnualReport_FINAL.pdf>

"Statistics for Family Businesses," American Management Services, Inc. <http://www.amserv.com/index. cfm/page/Family-Business-Statistics/pid/10715>

"U.S. Credit Union Profile: Year-End 2012 Summary of Credit Union Operating Results," Credit Union National Association, April, 2013 <http://www.cuna.org/Research-And-Strategy/Credit-Union-Data-And-Statistics/>

Women-Owned Businesses in the 21st Century," U.S. Department of Commerce Economics and Statistics Administration for the White House Council on Women and Girls, October 2010

2012 Global Reference Guide, Quirks Magazine, 2012

### *Succession*

Demasters, Karen, "Succession Survival Guide," Financial Advisor Magazine, June, 2012, <http://www.cassaday.com/documents/FAMagSuccessionArticleJune2012.pdf>

Gillia, Sean, "Succession Planning," U.S. Trust and Bank of America Private Wealth Management, Fall 2010, <http://www.ustrust.com/Publish/Content/application/pdf/GWMOL/Succession-Planning.pdf>

"Key person insurance can help companies mourning an owner," Insure.com, 28 May, 2009 <http://www.insu re.com/articles/business insurance/key-person-insurance.html

Merrill Lynch, "The Secrets to Succession," Merrill Lynch Bank of America Private Banking & Investment Group, Spring, 2012 <http://www.pbig.ml.com/pwa/pages/The-Secrets-to-Succession.aspx>

"The Pulse of Practice Health: an Insight into the Health of Elite Advisors' Firms," MultiFinancial Security Corporation, April, 2011, <https://s3.amazonaws.com/branch_production/uploads/resource/resource/1004/An_Insight_int o_the_Health_of_Elite_Advisors__Firms-White_Paper.pdf>

U.S. Trust, "2011 U.S. Trust Insights on Wealth and Worth," U.S. Trust and Bank of America Private Wealth Management, 2011, <http://www.ustrust.com/ Publish/Content/applica tion/ pdf/GWMOL/FactSheet.pdf>

# Endnotes

[1] "Kauffman FastFacts: Entrepreneurship and the Economy," Ewing Marian Kauffman Foundation, November, 2011 <<http://www.kauffman.org/uploadedfiles/factsheet/entrep_and_economy_fast_facts.pdf>

[2] Klein, Karen E., "Why Entrepreneurship Is Declining, Bloomberg Businessweek, 21 March, 2012, <http://www.businessweek.com/articles/2012-03-21/why-entrepreneurship-is-declining>

[3] "Kauffman FastFacts: Entrepreneurship and the Economy," Ewing Marian Kauffman Foundation, November, 2011 <<http://www.kauffman.org/uploadedfiles/factsheet/entrep_and_economy_fast_facts.pdf>

[4] Farrell, Chris, "Older Entrepreneurs Start Companies Too," Bloomberg Businessweek, 30 April, 2012, <http://www.businessweek.com/articles/2012-04-30/older-entrepreneurs-start-companies-too>

[5] "Kauffman FastFacts: Entrepreneurship and the Economy," Ewing Marian Kauffman Foundation, November, 2011 <<http://www.kauffman.org/uploadedfiles/factsheet/entrep_and_economy_fast_facts.pdf>

[6] Stangler, Dane, "The Coming Entrepreneurship Boom," Ewing Marion Kauffman Foundation, June 2009, p.4

[7] Farlie, Robert W., Kauffman Index of Entrepreneurial Activity, Ewing Marion Kauffman Foundation, 2012, p.4

[8] "National Women's Business Council 2012 Annual Report," National Women's Business Council, 2012, http://www.nwbc. gov/ites/default/files/NWBC_2012AnnualReport_FINAL.pdf>

[9] "Biz2Credit Analysis of Women-Owned Businesses Identifies Challenges for Female Entrepreneurs Seeking Small Business Loans," PRWire, 27 March, 2013, <<http://www.prweb.com/ releases/women/smallbusiness/prweb10573154.htm<

[10] National Women's Business Council 2012 Annual Report," National Women's Business Council, 2012, <http://www. nwbc.gov/sites/default/files/NWBC_2012AnnualReport_FINA L.pdf>

[11] National Women's Business Council 2012 Annual Report," National Women's Business Council, 2012, <http://www. nwbc.gov/sites/default/files/NWBC_2012AnnualReport_FINA L.pdf>

[12] "Biz2Credit Analysis of Women-Owned Businesses Identifies Challenges for Female Entrepreneurs Seeking Small Business Loans," PRWire, 27 March, 2013, <<http://www. prweb.com/releases/women/smallbusiness/prweb10573154. htm>

[13]"Biz2Credit Analysis of Women-Owned Businesses Identifies Challenges for Female Entrepreneurs Seeking Small Business Loans," PRWire, 27 March, 2013, <http://www.prweb.com/ releases/women/smallbusiness/prweb10573154.htm>

[14] "Federal Deposit Insurance Corporation (FDIC) Number of Institutions, Branches and Total Offices, FDIC-Insured Commercial Banks US and other Areas," 2012 <http://www2. fdic.gov/hsob/HSOBRpt.asp>

[15] "Community Banking Facts," Independent Community Bankers of America, March, 2012 <http://www.icba.org/ files/ICBASites/PDFs/cbfacts.pd>

[16] "U.S. Credit Union Profile: Year-End 2012 Summary of Credit Union Operating Results," Credit Union National

Association, April, 2013 <http://www.cuna.org/Research-And-Strategy/Credit-Union-Data-And-Statistics/>

[17] National Venture Capital Association Yearbook 2012, National Venture Capital Association, Thompson Reuters) p.7

[18] "By the Numbers." Private Equity Growth Capital Council, 2012 http://www.pegcc.org/education/pe-by-the-numbers/

[19] Koetsier, John, "The rise of the angel investor (infographic)," Venture Beat/Entrepreneur, 19 February, 2013, http://venturebeat.com/2013/02/19/the-rise-of-the-angel-investor-infographic/

[20] Sudek, Richard, May, Allan, Wiltbank, Robert, "Angel Investing: Catalyst for Innovation," October, 2011

[21] Master, Marc, "Business plans and their importance and 78% of businesses do not have one," Examiner.com, 22May, 2010, <http://www.examiner.com/article/ business-plans-and-their-importance-and-78%-of-businesses-do-not-have-one>

[22] Blank, Steve, "Part I: Validate Your Business Model Start with a Business Model, Not a Business Plan," The Wall Street Journal/The Accelerators, 26 November, 2012, <http://blogs.wsj.com/accelerators/2012/11/26/start-with-a-business-model-not-a-business-plan/>

[23] Blank, Steve, "Part I: Validate Your Business Model Start with a Business Model, Not a Business Plan," The Wall Street Journal/The Accelerators, 26 November, 2012, <http://blogs.wsj.com/accelerators/2012/11/26/start-with-a-business-model-not-a-business-plan/>

[24] Kerin, Roger A., Hartley, Steven W., Rudelius, William, Marketing (McGraw-Hill Irvwin, 2013) p.235

[25] "Frequently Asked Questions about Small Business," U.S. Small Business Administration, September, 2012

[26] Dun & Bradstreet. (2011). The State of Small Businesses Post Great Recession: An Analysis of Small Businesses

between 2007 and 2011. <http://www.dnbgov.com/pdf/ DNB_SMB_Report_May2011.pdf>

[27] National Venture Capital Association Yearbook 2012, National Venture Capital Association, (Thompson Reuters)

[28] National Venture Capital Association Yearbook 2012, National Venture Capital Association, 2012 (Thompson Reuters 2012)

[29] MacQueen, Evan, Vice-President of Core Capital Partners. Personal interview, March, 2013.

[30] McGovern, Mark, CEO, MobileSystem7. Personal interview, April, 2013.

[31] Kaplan, Steve A., corporate attorney, Pillsbury, Winthrop, Shaw, Pitman. Personal interview, March, 2013.

[32] Glass, Noah, founder and CEO, OLO Online Ordering. Personal interview, April, 2013.

[33] Lagorio, Christine, "9 Questions to Ask a Small Business Lender," Inc., 6 May, 2010 <http;//www.inc.com/guides/ 2010/05/9-discussions-to-have-with-your-banker-lender. html>

[34] Wilson, Steven, "Commerical loans available for well-prepared businesses," Dayton Business Journal, 26 April, 2010 <http://www.bizjournals.com/dayton/stories/2010/ 04/26/story6.html>

[35] Kruse, Kevin, "Zig Ziglar: 10 Quotes That Can Change Your Life," Forbes, 28 November, 2012, <http://www.forbes.com/ sites/kevinkruse/2012/11/28/zig-ziglar-10-quotes-that-can-change-your-life/>

[36] Shah, Darmesh, Inbound Marketing: Get Found Using Google, Social Media and Blogs, (John Wiley & Sons, Inc., 2009)

[37] 2012 Global Reference Guide, Research Now and Quirks Magazine, 2012

[38] Fenn, Donna, "10 Ways to Get More Sales From Existing Customers," INC., 31 August, 2010, <http://www.inc.com/guides/2010/08/get-more-sales-from-existing-customers.html>

[39] Reichheld, Frederick, F., "The Economics of E Loyalty," Harvard Business School, 10 July, 2000, <http://hbswk.hbs.edu/archive/1590.html>

[40] Drucker, Peter F. , Management: Tasks, Responsibilities, Practices (HarperBusiness 1993) p.119

[41] Domingo, Rene T., "True Productivity: The Key to Profitability," RTDonline, 2003

[42] Domingo, Rene T., "True Productivity: The Key to Profitability," RTDonline, 2003

[43] Reichheld, Frederick F., Sasser, W. Earl, Jr., "Zero Defections: Quality Comes to Services," Harvard Business Review September 1990 <http://hbr.org/1990/09/zero-defections-quality-comes-to-services/ar/1>

[44] Murphy, Emmett c., Murphy, Mark A., "Leading on the Edge of Chaos: The 10 Critical Elements for Success in Volatile Times," (Prentice Hall Press 2002)

[45] Tomic, Nancy. "Customer Satisfaction Statistics," <http://nancytomic.blogspot.com/2013/03/why-do-customers-leave-statistics.html>

[46] "The Mystery of Disappearing Customers," Adviceinice, <http://www.adviceinice.com/main7.cfm?id=467B70F7-E0AB-8438-C72EB0DCEE73CF93>

[47] RightNow, "Customer Experience Report: North America 2010," RightNow Technologies, 2011 <http://www.rightnow.com/files/analyst-reports/RightNow-Customer-Experience-Impact-North-America-Report.pdf>

[48] "22 Really Useful Customer Retention Statistics," Customer Thermometer, <http://www.slideshare.net/custthermometer/22-customer-retention-stats>

[49] Allen, James, Reichheld, Frederick, Hamilton, Barney, "Closing the Delivery Gap: How to Achieve True Customer-led Growth," Bain & Company Inc., 2005, <http://www.bain.com/bainweb/pdfs/cms/hottopics/closingdeliverygap.pdf>

[50] "22 Really Useful Customer Retention Statistics," Customer Thermometer, <http://www.slideshare.net/ custthermometer /22-customer-retention-stats>

[51] Hayes, Mark, "Stop Obsessing Over Revenue: 3 Proven Strategies for Increasing Profitability," Shopify, 4 October, 2012, < http://www.shopify.com/blog/6657676-stop-obsessing-over-revenue-3-proven-strategies-for-increasing-profitability#axzz2XZ2vdShZ>

[52] "22 Really Useful Customer Retention Statistics," Customer Thermometer, <http://www.slideshare.net/custthermometer/22-customer-retention-stats>

[53] Hayes, Mark, "Stop Obsessing Over Revenue: 3 Proven Strategies for Increasing Profitability," Shopify, 4 October, 2012, < http://www.shopify.com/blog/6657676-stop-obsessing-over-revenue-3-proven-strategies-for-increasing-profitability#axzz2XZ2vdShZ>

[54] Porter, Michael E., Competitive Strategy: Techniques for Analyzing Industries and Competitors ,(Free Press, 1998)

[55] Porter, Michael E., Competitive Strategy: Techniques for Analyzing Industries and Competitors ,(Free Press, 1998)

[56] U.S. Trust, "2011 U.S. Trust Insights on Wealth and Worth," U.S. Trust and Bank of America Private Wealth Management, 2011 <http://www.ustrust.com/Publish/Content/application/pdf/GWMOL/FactSheet.pdf>

[57] "Frequently Asked Questions about Small Business," U.S. Small Business Administration, September, 2012

[58] McPeak, Isabella, "Family Business Statistics in the US," Peak Family Business, 25 October, 2011 <http://peak familybusiness.com/2011/10/25/family-business-statistics-in-the-us/>

[59] Gillia, Sean, "Succession Planning," U.S. Trust and Bank of America Private Wealth Management, Fall 2010, <http://www.ustrust.com/Publish/Content/application/pdf/GWMOL/Succession-Planning.pdf>

[60] "The Pulse of Practice Health: an Insight into the Health of Elite Advisors' Firms," MultiFinancial Security Corporation, April, 2011 <https://s3.amazonaws.com/ branch_ production /uploads/resource/resource/1004/An_Insight_into_the_Health_of_Elite_Advisors__Firms-White_Paper.pdf>

[61] "Key Person Insurance can Help Companies Mourning an Owner or Executive," Insure.com, 28May, 2009, <http://www.insure.com/articles/businessinsurance/key-person-insurance.html>

[62] Maltby, Emily, "More Owners Help Finance Sales of Their Firms," The Wall Street Journal, 8 March, 2012

[63] Federal Reserve System, Report to Congress on Availability of Credit to Small Business, 2012

[64] "In FTC Study, Five Percent of Consumers Had Errors On Their Credit Reports That Could Result in Less Favorable Terms for Loans," Federal Trade Commission, 11 February, 2013, <http://www.ftc.opa/2013/02/creditreport.shtm>

[65] National Small Business Association, Small Business Access to Capital Survey, 2012, <http://www.nsba.biz/wp-content/uploads/2012/07/access-to-capital-survey.pdf>

[66] Small Business Administration, "7(a) Loan Repayment Terms," U.S. Small Business Administration, <http://www.sba.gov/content/7a-loan-repayment-terms>

[67] Markowitz, Eric, "5 Tips for Using Collateral to Secure a Small Business Loan," INC., 31 January, 2001, <http://www.

inc.com/guides/201101/5-tips-using-collateral-to-secure-a-small-business-loan.html>

[68] Cunningham, Simon, "P2P Lending Sites: An Exhaustive Review," Lending Memo, 7 May, 2002, http://www.lending memo.com/p2p-lending-sites/

[69] Hall, Alan E., "Don't Abandon Crowdfunding—Manage It," Harvard Business Review Blog Network, 10 May, 2012, http://blogs.hbr.org/cs/2012/05/crowdfunding_is_a_critical_res.html

[70] Clark, Patrick, "Crowdfunders are Quietly Donating and Lending Billions," BloombergBusinessweek, 8 April, 2013 <http://www.businessweek.com/articles/2013-04-08/crowd funders-are-quietly-donating-and-lending-billions>

[71] Hall, Alan E., "Don't Abandon Crowdfunding—Manage It," Harvard Business Review Blog Network, 10 May, 2012, <http://www.blogs.hbr.org/cs/2012/05/crowdfunding-is-a-critical.res>

[72] Brooks, Rich, "11 Tips for Crowdfunding: How to Raise Money from Strangers," SocialMedia Examiner, 14 September, 2011, <http://www.socialmediaexaminer.com/11-tips for-crowdfunding-how-to-raise-money-from-strangers/>

[73] Strauss, Steven D., Get Your Business Funded: Creative Methods for Getting the Funding You Need (John Wiley & Sons, Inc., 2011), p. 87.

[74] Kerin, Roger A., Hartley, Steven W., Rudelius, William, Marketing (McGraw-Hill Irwin, 2013), p. 220.

[75] Kerin, Roger A., Hartley, Steven W., Rudelius, William, Marketing (McGraw-Hill Irwin, 2013), p. 227.

[76] Kerin, Roger A., Hartley, Steven W., Rudelius, William, Marketing (McGraw-Hill Irwin, 2013), p. 235.

# Index

# *For More Information*

Website: www.WeklarBusinessInstitute.com

Winning Business Financing Blog:
www.WeklarBusinessInstitute.com/blog

Upcoming Programs:
www.WeklarBusinessInstitute.com/events

Facebook:
www.facebook.com/WeklarBusinessInstitute
www.facebook.com/MasteringTheMoneyMaze

LinkedIn:
www.linkedin.com/in/dianeweklar

Twitter:
www.twitter.com/dianeweklar

www.ingramcontent.com/pod-product-compliance
Lightning Source LLC
Chambersburg PA
CBHW060323200326
41519CB00011BA/1817